PRA
TRAINING FOR THI

MW00937013

We read the first chapter and moved ~~to tears. Our spiritual~~ son, Eddie Mason, has written a profoundly moving book, opening his heart honestly and allowing us to look inside. What we see is ourselves. None of us can self-correct. We desperately need a playbook for our lives. We plan to read this book again, and share it with the people that we love, so that together we can win the tough game of life.

CHESTER & MARION MITCHELL. Sr. Pastor of Capital Community Church, Ashburn, Virginia and Author of *The Healing Road To Heaven: Walking With God From Pain To Peace*

Eddie Mason's *Training for the Tough Game of Life* is a compelling journey of overcoming personal adversity from calling bad plays. By discovering a life-transforming 'playbook,' he learned to make the right calls. Inspiring, riveting, and enlightening, this is a must read if you want to succeed in life.

TROY VINCENT. NFL, Vice President of Football Operations...and NFL Legend

Eddie Mason, who was a starting linebacker for us at UNC has written a must read book for all. It teaches us how to turn a crisis into a positive. Your life will be better with this read. As always, I'm so proud of Eddie. Thanks for sharing your thoughts and your life with us, my friend!

MACK BROWN. UNC & Texas University Head Football Coach 2005 BCS National Champions

In *Training for the Tough Game of Life*, Coach Eddie Mason comes along side you with God's playbook and passionately shows you how to overcome your life obstacles. But this is much more than a training manual. Coach Eddie is living it. With honesty and vulnerability, he takes you through his own tough times, walking you through God's playbook for his own life, bringing you face-to-face with the wisdom he has gained on the field of life. If you are in the pain of life and losing your grip, pick up this training manual now, read it, apply it, and let Coach Eddie coach take you forward through your tough time and across the goal line!

CRAIG MOORMAN, PH.D., Founder and Director, Finding Solutions Counseling Centers

GUIDANCE AND HELP FROM GOD'S PLAYBOOK

TRAINING
FOR THE
TOUGH GAME
OF LIFE

EDDIE MASON

Training for the Tough Game of Life

©2015 by Eddie Mason

Unless otherwise noted, scripture quotations are from the *Holy Bible*, New Living Translation, (NLT) copyright ©1996, 2004, 2007 by Tyndale House Foundation. Used by permission of Tyndale House Publishers, Inc., Carol Stream, Illinois 60188. All rights reserved.

Scripture quotations identified as NIV are taken from *The Holy Bible, New International Version*® NIV®. Copyright © 1973, 1978, 1984, 2011 by Biblica, Inc.™ Used by permission of Zondervan. All rights reserved worldwide. www.zondervan.com. The "NIV" and "New International Version" are trademarks registered in the United States Patent and Trademark Office by Biblica, Inc.™

Scripture quotations identified ESV are from The Holy Bible, English Standard Version® (ESV®), copyright 2001 by Crossway, a publishing ministry of Good News Publishers. Used by permission. All rights reserved. ESV Text Edition: 2007.

Scripture quotations identified NKJ are taken from *The Holy Bible*, New King James Version. Copyright © 1979, 1980, 1982 by Thomas Nelson, Inc. Used by permission. All rights reserved.

Library of Congress Cataloging-in-Publication Data
Mason, Eddie
        Training for the Tough Game of Life / Eddie Mason
p. cm.

ISBN 978-1-50759-352-3

Printed in the United States of America
21 20 19 18 17 16 15 (CS) 10 9 8 7 6 5 4 3 2 1

Design by Peter Gloege | LOOK Design Studio

Editorial development and creative design support by Ascent:
www.itsyourlifebethere.com

Follow Eddie Mason:

 Eddie.L.Mason1   www.CoachMason.org

*I dedicate this book to
those who have been broken
by the game of life
and have found courage, faith, hope
and love again to not be afraid
to allow God to pick up the pieces
and help you get back in
the Tough Game of Life.*

CONTENTS

ACKNOWLEDGMENTS

To my wife, Sonya who knows me better than anyone. Who has seen me at my worst and my best and still allowed God to show you my heart and give you patience to wait as He worked on me. You are more than a wife, but a friend, and one who I can truly place my confidence and trust in. You truly have my heart! For that I am eternally grateful to you. To my kids, Tyler, Sydney and Elisha—You are the best kids a father could ever have. To our grandparents, moms, dads, brothers and sisters and family who have been with us through it all. To my spiritual family on many levels, who have walked with Sonya and I all these years. My mentors, brothers and friends who helped sharpen me to become the man I am today, not yesterday. A special thank you to Pastor Chester L. Mitchell and Marion Mitchell for being a great spiritual mom and dad. My two mentors in Pastor Chad Carlton and Dr. Craig Morman, Thank you! To David Hazard for being a constant force of encouragement on this literary work. To Karen for believing in the work and doing the necessary editing to help me sharpen the book. To Jesus Christ for redeeming me from myself and helping me to look myself in the mirror not at the reflection of what I saw, but at the possibility of what I could become!

"*For I know the plans*

I have for you declares the Lord,

plans to prosper you

and not to harm you,

plans to give you

hope and a future."

JEREMIAH 29:11

CHAPTER ONE

REALIZING WE ALL NEED A PLAYBOOK

MY LIFE WAS changed forever in the summer of 1977 when I was just five years old. This was a time without a care, when I should have been enjoying playing outside in the country humid air of Siler City, North Carolina. Instead, I found myself thrust into an atmosphere that would literally lay the framework of how I would struggle playing the game of life out for the next twenty-plus years.

I was playing outside my mom's and dad's trailer home with my Tonka truck, dreaming of driving a big truck, when in reality I was simply pushing along the rich soil I had somehow plowed up. It was at that moment that I heard my mother's voice cry for help. I knew this voice, for it was the voice I had heard since I was a baby. I heard another voice that was angry, passionate, and had reached its boiling point and was about to do something that would be a major regret. I had heard these sounds before, and most times I had ignored them.

But this was not like any other. This time it was different, from the standpoint that I heard an undertone in my mom's voice that exuded fear and that her life was on the line. Even at five I knew something was not right! I tried to ignore it, as I was engrossed in my normal activity of playing by myself in the backyard. This was my way of escaping the screams and yells that I was accustomed to and in most instances had become numb to.

I ran to my mom's voice and realized my dad and mom were in a very serious and escalated argument.

I grabbed my father's leg as he held my mother by her hair with the intent to hit her, but I somehow instinctively grabbed his leg and began to bite him. This was enough to get him to release my mother and turn his focus to me, his youngest son, the one who kept to himself and was simply happy to be playing in the backyard.

My dad grabbed me and flung me as I attempted to hold on, but I was able to free my mom from the grasp of his large hand. For a brief moment there was silence as my dad realized he had hit his five-year-old son. There was not an apology, nor did the fight stop; instead, there was a mere pause where my eyes met his and I saw the anger, hurt, pain, and frustration that he did not know how to communicate except through the abuse of his hands, voice, and bottle. It was at this moment I realized that his addiction was his pain. It was not over; it was only beginning. He proceeded to attack my mom and the only thing that saved her was my Grandma Emma, who had come and stood at the door unwavering, daring my dad to come past her.

His spirit was subdued and he became very silent and just walked away, dejected, realizing what he had done.

Looking back at that moment, I realize everyone has a playbook for playing the game of life. People play the game of life out through abuse, addiction, pain, unforgiveness, or loss of hope, trying their best to gain ground toward a greater sense of worth that leads to a brighter future.

SPIRITUAL TRUTH: *Jesus looked at them and said, 'With man this is impossible, but with God all things are possible.' (Matthew 19:26)*

These people use the pain they have battled through in the game of life as fuel to get them from one quarter to the next, never stopping for a moment to consider the rules they are breaking, the penalties they are causing, and the fouls that are hurting others along the way. They never stop for a moment to consider that there is a greater playbook in God's Word that can give them better options for how to have great success. We have to ask ourselves the real question: Which playbook are we using? Are we still running plays based on our will or His?

Are we playing this game called life based on the pain of our past or a bad life decision we made that still has us dejected or allowing hurts to hinder us from moving forward to the life in God's promise? The intent of this book is to help you understand that everyone has a playbook and we all have to make calls, but the outcome in the game of life will be based on our ability to make the right calls God's way.

CHAPTER 2

NEW BEGINNINGS

IMMEDIATELY AFTER that huge fight we moved out from the chaos of my father's house and went from one extreme to the other—from fighting to faith. It was a big adjustment and exactly what we needed as a family. We had longed for a peace that, as long as I could remember, I had never experienced. This was the day my mother gave birth to faith that would launch us into the first quarter of a life journey to trust God. The moment she saw my dad put his hands on me, my mother gained the strength to determine that we could not go another day in that environment.

Suddenly, everything was happening so fast. "Get your things!" she yelled. What does a five-year-old grab? His Tonka truck in the back yard, his toys, clothes...what?

As upset as she was, my mom instructed us to grab the necessary items, but I would never let go of my Tonka truck, as it was the one thing close to home that I was able to carry. My mother's wounded voice would carry the burden of labor and pain to sacrifice for the benefit of her children. She would live in this place for many years, never revisiting or discussing THE DAY that changed our destinies and family dynamic forever!

My mom had decided that her playbook for life would be silence amidst the pain to regain a voice that had been lost through the abuse of her past.

This was the day that we moved from a chaotic environment to one of faith and peace. Although my grandmother was a very outspoken woman who shared her opinion regularly, living with her was the best thing that could have happened. The painful and sometimes unbearable atmosphere that we had been so accustomed to as normal had been left behind in favor of faith, hope, love, compassion, and kindness. Mom decided that she was not going to play by dad's playbook anymore but her own, which would take time to figure out.

SPIRITUAL TRUTH: *For the Lord has not given me the spirit of fear, but of power love and a sound mind. (2 Timothy 2:7)*

Sometimes life can present some fourth-and-one situations where your back is against the wall and there seems to be no way out, but you have to rely on the power that rests in God in order to choose the right path. Not living in fear, but resting and relying on faith that conquers all fear. This is exactly what my mom and our family did.

As we were loading the car, I could hear my mother under her breath saying, "Jesus, Jesus, Jesus, Jesus!" She continued to repeat his name, and every time she called that name as we sat in the car with tears in our eyes, it brought more and more peace. She kept saying it, as if to cry out to the Lord saying, "Lord help us!" It was a statement and a prayer that was drawing a line of separation between the pain of her past and the hope of the new future we were starting. Although the game of life was presenting a new set of plays we had not seen before, it was very evident that mom was clear that it was time for a halftime adjustment. It was time to give our family a fresh breath of air for the next drive ahead. God had given us a new set of downs and it was our time to take it and run with it.

SPIRITUAL TRUTH: *Remember not the former things, nor consider the things of old. Behold, I was doing a new thing; now it springs forth, do you not perceive it? I will make a way in the wilderness and rivers in the desert. (Isaiah 43: 18–19)*

CHAPTER 3

BATTLING THE PAIN OF YOUR PAST

EVEN AS MY MOM had made many adjustments, I was left as a five-year-old to make many of my own. As we left my old home and were forced to move into a new one, I had no idea what to expect. My mind was racing, trying to figure out just how this life was going to be. There were so many emotions, things that I did not understand, things I wanted answers to and questions I had but was afraid to ask because I feared the response.

> **SPIRITUAL TRUTH:** *Be strong and courageous. Do not be afraid or terrified because of them, for the Lord your God goes with you; he will never leave you nor forsake you. (Deuteronomy 31:6)*

So we pull up to my grandparent's home, which was literally one mile away. My Grandfather walked out on the porch in his patent bib overalls and made no gestures, just made a peaceful, yet stern face that said, "Come on in, family," as if to reassure us that everything was going to be okay. His face and demeanor represented safety. But isn't it ironic how safety can be so close, but so far away.

SPIRITUAL TRUTH: *Where no wise guidance is, the people falleth; But in the multitude of counsellors there is safety. (Proverbs 11:14)*

We got out of the car. No one said a word. It was the most silence I had experienced in my entire life. All I knew was that the place we left would never be our home again. But even though we had left the place, the pain of my past was still there. The moment we got out of the car, there was so much emotion and the shock of what just happened was still there. I started crying but tried my best to hold back my tears so as to not upset my mother. She saw me and gave me a hug, and my grandfather picked me up and carried me in the house and sat me in his chair. "Son," he said, "you are safe now. This will never happen to you again." I felt so reassured and at peace that I fell asleep, exhausted from the emotion of that day. I would later arise and resume life as usual, grabbing my Tonka truck and going outside to play. It was the one thing that made life normal for me. That is what we try to find during times of trial; anything that makes us feel normal. When I played with my truck, I was able to escape all the raw emotion that I felt and in reality could not possibly understand as a five-year-old. I tried to imagine life differently, but because of all the painful experiences I had become accustomed to, the physical sounds of abuse in my ears now moved to screams in my head.

SPIRITUAL TRUTH: *How long must I wrestle with my thoughts and day after day have sorrow in my heart? How long will my enemy triumph over me? (Psalms 13:2)*

This created a problem: I wanted the noises out. I wanted the yells and screams out. I wanted the pain to stop, but what does a five-year-old do? There was nothing I could do. The wrestling with the voices inside my head persisted. I tried to imagine a better life, but I kept hearing my dad say, "You will die before I let go of your mom." As that thought replayed in my head, it sent chills through me, and although we were free of the physical abuse, the mental, emotional, and spiritual damage was already done.

I had hoped that what my grandfather and mother were telling me would actually happen, but pain is powerful in the hands and minds of the brokenhearted. I thought it would stop, but it never did. I was left to figure out how to deal with this recurring playbook in the game life that up to this point had dealt me some very bad plays. There was no way I could have ever prepared myself at the age of five to deal with all these circumstances that we were thrust into, simply as a product of pain.

So just like my dad, who was obviously full of anger, resentment, and unforgiveness, I, too, started to live my life with the only attitude I knew. The voices of ridicule and turmoil that I had hoped would disappear magically and never come back only got worse. So I made a decision to start playing the plays in the game of life with the pain, medicating them with emotions of suppression and seclusion from the pain of my past.

CHAPTER 4

SECLUSION & SUPPRESSION

AS I GOT OLDER, I started to learn how to cover up my emotions through suppression and seclusion, but I was also taking much of my anger out on my friends during games and on my toys when I played. My behavior was turning from fun-loving to very destructive. Although I could not have known it at that time, this would be the very thing that would mold the nature and character of who I would eventually become.

SPIRITUAL TRUTH: *For as he thinks in his heart, so is he. (Proverbs 23:7)*

The game of life had taught me how to take "bad mental repetitions" from the pain of my past. The only way I knew to respond is not to show emotion or express how I felt. Suppressing how I felt and secluding myself from the truth is what made me feel okay. I just wanted these voices out of my head, but in some strange way, they were what really made me feel normal.

So I made up my mind to accept that I would have to live with the voices in my head—the screams, yells, violent behavior, abuse, alcoholic rants and raves, the nights running outside, and the nightmares of my past. Although this was not the right way, it was the best way for me to cope with all the damage that had been done to me emotionally. I chose to bury it, never realizing the pain would resurface and present itself again, but this time in a much greater way.

> **SPIRITUAL TRUTH:** *Then it goes and takes with it seven other spirits more wicked than itself, and they go in and live there. And the final condition of that person is worse than the first. That is how it will be with this wicked generation. (Matthew 12:45)*

It was around the age of eight that I started to develop an ability to "play through pain" and use whatever emotion available to get me through to the next day. This would all be tested that summer, when my cousin Lamont came to visit. He was a rambunctious dude, full of life, and he loved to compete. He came to my house and asked, "Do you wanna play?" In my heart I wanted to, but the fear of rejection, simply not knowing how to communicate, made me clam up. I looked at him and although I really did not want to play, I said, "Yes, I'll come out and play." I was afraid, not of my cousin, but of him asking me things I did not know how to answer. So I rethought my answer and said, "You go ahead, and I will catch up later." I was making up every kind of excuse to avoid playing and risking the opportunity of him asking me a question I did not want to answer. I simply did not want to open myself up. My cousin said, "Please come out when you get a chance. I want to play."

I had not realized that although God had set us free from that abusive environment, I was still a prisoner to the emotion of the pain that lived inside my head. Staying secluded really felt in that moment like the safest place to be. My cousin had no idea of the struggles I had, and I surely was not going to tell him that I was simply AFRAID. Again, I was not afraid of my cousin, but I was afraid of the idea of opening my heart up again and wanted to avoid the pain of being rejected, feeling like I was not worthy, or risking the chance of not living up to the standard of my cousin's expectations. All of this was in my head, as my cousin never knew where I was emotionally and spiritually. How many of us go through the game of life worried, living in fear and focused on things that don't even exist? We spend more time being anxious and focused on things that are of no importance at this point in the game of life. Yet we will continue to allow ourselves to wrestle internally, never being able to move forward.

I did not know at that time why I took the step of faith to go play with him, but I did learn this: Playing in the game of life oftentimes is about having a willingness to take the first step. About looking at the present moment of opportunity to get you beyond your past. So we went outside and we started to ride our bikes, which was a true love and passion of mine. Although I had never told anyone that, I let my cousin know through my excitement and passion as we jumped hills at our Aunt Lillian's house. We rode and rode on the hot, humid dirt roads, then stopped for a drink of water from Aunt Lillian's well. He had somehow got me, the secluded and suppressed eight year old, to come out of my shell. He had coached me off the sidelines of life back onto the field of play and restored my heart to live again. Having so much fun that day taught me that if you do not enjoy what you do, you will always sit right where you are, allowing the fear to quench the fire of the unlimited possibilities that God is trying to show you. Take the first step out of seclusion and suppression into the unlimited God presently has for you!

That summer was the best I had ever had, and I have to thank God for using my cousin Lamont to help me see life as it is, not what it was.

CHAPTER 5

GREAT LOSS

I LEARNED SO MUCH from the experiences that summer with my cousin. I learned that it was okay to be yourself, to open up and not feel afraid to let others know how you feel. Although the internal scars were still there, life had become so much more manageable, and my heart and mind had begun to heal. Even though it appeared that on the surface everything was okay, I had no idea what was about to happen. Just at the time when the game of life had given me a time-out to regroup and refocus, the greatest trial of my life happened.

It was a typical Saturday morning when my grandfather and I had gotten up to go clean the stockyard. He called out to me at his normal four a.m. early rise, knocking on the door of my bedroom, saying, "Eddie, it is time to go." I responded, "Okay Grandpa." I was so sleepy and, to be quite honest, did not want to get up. The big difference between living with my dad and living with my grandpa was discipline. My grandfather did not compromise his relationship with God or his work ethic.

SPIRITUAL TRUTH: *And he answering said, Thou shalt love the Lord thy God with all thy heart, and with all thy soul, and with all thy strength, and with all thy mind; and thy neighbor as thyself. (Luke 10:27)*

I walked out the door and started heading toward my papa's Buick. As soon as I got inside the car, grandpa started to tell me what we had to do today at the stockyard. Now, the stockyard was papa's side job. I considered myself his trusted assistant and took pride in my job. As we started to drive, grandpa said, "Today, son, I am going to need you to clean the bathrooms, sweep the catwalk, and ensure that all the trash cans are emptied." I said, "I will take care of it papa." He just smiled, as if to say I know you will. We finally arrived at the stockyard. I can tell you this one thing after working there for so long: it was the smelliest place on earth. Stinky pigs, cows, and horses were housed for sale in an all-indoor facility. But that was not the reason I loved getting up every Saturday at 4:30 am; it was because I loved being with my grandpa.

SPIRITUAL TRUTH: *You will be secure, because there is hope; you will look about you and take your rest in safety. (Job 11:18)*

From the first day we pulled up to his house many years ago and he was standing there as a mighty warrior, grandpa had become my rock and hero. He was the one I looked up to, and I could never get enough time with him. But on this day, there was a calm and peace in the air as we went to work at the stockyard. I had my window down; I loved to have my hand out the window and let the air run through my fingers. Our routine every Saturday was for me to ask my, "Papa can I have a snack?"

He responded, "Yes son, but only one." He gave me the change I needed, which was twenty-five cents, and this really made my day. It seems like such a small thing, but it was really a big deal for me. I was in seventh heaven. I tried not to be overly excited, but inside I was bubbling. We got back into the old Green Buick and started to drive home. I did not have a care in the world with my hand out the window, the honey bun I had bought from the snack machine, and a big smile on my face. As we headed home I could only think about how happy I was and how much things were different now.

But just like only the game of life can do, there was a new set of downs and challenges ahead that I had no way of planning or being prepared for. As we made the left turn down the big curve headed home to papa's house, I noticed a lot of cars. I immediately looked at my grandpa for assurance and asked him, "What's going on papa?" He looked back at me and said, "I don't know, son." As we got closer my heart started to race and although I was not that old, my discernment was very strong and I had this feeling in my gut that something was not right. Tons of cars were parked alongside the highway. This could only mean one of two things: someone had died, or someone had been born. My heart sank, my mind started racing, and the anxiousness and fear that had taken so long to overcome started to raise its head again.

> **SPIRITUAL TRUTH**: *Comforted His people with these words, 'But now thus says the LORD, he who created you, O Jacob, he who formed you, O Israel: Fear not, for I have redeemed you; I have called you by name, you are mine. When you pass through the waters, I will be with you; and through the rivers, they shall not overwhelm you; when you walk through fire you shall not be burned, and the flame shall not consume you.' (Isaiah 43:1–2 ESV).*

My life had begun to heal, but as soon as we parked, I realized this life of peace would soon turn right back to one of pain. I ran into the house, not really knowing what to expect, but knowing that whatever was happening was not going to be good. Although it could have easily been something positive, my short game-time experience in life had been so negative that I did not know how to expect anything else than the worst. That is exactly what happened, as my mom revealed to me that my older brother had died in a tragic car accident.

I did not understand. I could not wrap my head around him being gone. He was my best friend, the one person beyond my grandpa I looked up too. So many questions ran through my head. What did that look like, did that mean he was never coming back...what? So many questions, but the pain within my heart made me so angry. I questioned all the good God was doing and decided to trade it in for the pain of my past. I was emotionally done and had hit my bottom. I was empty and there was no one in that house in the midst of the tears who could help me. I kneeled down at my bed and cried until my eyes were swollen almost shut. My mom came in to try to console me. She said, "Eddie, what can I do son?" I said, "Nothing!" In reality there is nothing anyone could do. The layers of pain I felt were almost unbearable and heavy! The weight of pain I was carrying had disabled and incapacitated my spirit. I put the game on pause and all the emotions that came along with what had happened. I was numb to my present, absent from the pain of past, and had no interest in the hope of my future. I wanted to die. I did not want life anymore, because it seemed like every time I started to attempt to get the confidence to go back into the game of life, something else would come to knock me back down on the sidelines of life.

Trying to sort through the loss of my brother was difficult enough, as I simply did not know how to contend with the emotional battle that life was playing out in front of me. It was as if I had gotten behind in the game of life, was trying to make a comeback, and then had suffered a turnover that could cost me the game.

> **SPIRITUAL TRUTH:** *What do you do when your way of playing the game of life is simply not working? When the tactic of putting on the face of pride, staying in seclusion, and bottling up the emotions was no longer a play I could run? I had tried to keep my composure throughout all the difficult years of abuse, but this time I could not contain myself. God was allowing the trying times of my life to reveal the true nature of who I really was. It was time for me to address the frailty and reality of where I was, which was avoiding and acting as though everything was fine. God knew that this pain, if not addressed, would cost me in the end if I were unwilling to look at where I truly was.*

So I started to lean on what I knew best when I was experiencing defeat: To walk in silence and not communicate my emotions. Anger, resentment and unforgiveness were building all the while, and there was no way I could know that all the trials from the abuse, the move, and the death of my brother would start to deteriorate my confidence and faith in God. I wanted to believe, but the trials and lack of confidence just would not allow me to. So I started to look for confidence in people, places, and things instead of looking for it in God.

LIFE TRUTH: *Thus says the Lord: Cursed is the man who trusts in man and makes flesh his strength, whose heart turns away from the Lord. He is like a shrub in the desert, and shall not see any good come. He shall dwell in the parched places of the wilderness, in an uninhabited salt land. Blessed is the man who trusts in the Lord, whose trust is the Lord. He is like a tree planted by water, that sends out its roots by the stream, and does not fear when heat comes, for its leaves remain green, and is not anxious in the year of drought, for it does not cease to bear fruit. The heart is deceitful above all things, and desperately sick; who can understand it? (Jeremiah 17: 5–12)*

My brother's death would prove more costly than just a great loss. It would be the very thing that would cause my heart to harden again.

CHAPTER 6

KNOCKED DOWN, BUT NOT OUT

BY HIGH SCHOOL, out of all the bad experiences I had up to that point, football seemed to be the one thing that was going well. I was getting used to the daily rigors of practice and was really starting to enjoy it. Each day as I would get up for practice, especially the first couple of days, it appeared that all was perfect—until we put on the pads for the first time. Up to now, we had just been in shorts and shoulder pads, with no one being allowed to tackle. We had gone over techniques for each position, over and over. Coach Senter was such a stickler for detail, and he would yell over and over, "Keep your head up, no arm tackling, and run your feet on contact." Well, doing this on a pad is one thing, but doing it on a live person is another, because that person is moving. But Coach Senter would not let it go. He wanted it done right, and just as we would finish one drill, he would start another to continue to help us ensure our safety and that we were getting better.

SPIRITUAL TRUTH: *Whatever your hand finds to do, do it with all your might. (Ecclesiastes 9:10)*

Coach Senter wanted everything to be perfect, with attention to detail down to the smallest thing. I did not realize at that moment in my life that he was not just teaching us how to play the game of football—he was teaching us how to play the game of life. Not only that, but he was instilling a mindset that would carry on for me personally for years to come. He would not compromise on doing things to perfection for anyone. His intent was on making sure we did things to his standard and not our own. In all honesty, if you are going to have someone in your life, you want the right people who will raise the standard, in order that you can envision and see yourself as better than where you are.

But this day would present more than just another day in football; that day, I learned a very valuable life lesson I would never forget. It was like any other day at football practice, except we could feel the anticipation of our first full contact practice. Some players had done this many times, but it was my first time experiencing the high energy and alpha-male mindset of being in that locker room with all my teammates as they got pumped up. The great thing is that I had the comfort of two of my best friends, Ryan and Glen, to share this experience with. They had played before, so they did not look at all intimidated. Glen looked over at me and said "Eddie, you ready bro?" I responded, "Heck yeah man! Ready to go, bro!" But down deep inside of me was this gut-wrenching feeling of nervous energy, and I was thinking, "What did I just get myself into?" We joked back and forth with one another about who would hit harder, but it was only talk. All of us were scared to death, but we put on this face of security, as if to demonstrate to one another that we were unfazed by the fact that this was the first day of contact.

> **LIFE TRUTH:** *How many of us have been in a situation where we are scared to death and are afraid to admit it, because we are worried about what people will think?*

Well, that is exactly where I was and what I was feeling, and it would have been ten times easier simply to tell someone how I was feeling instead of trying to carry around this macho ego that was still this scared little boy who was trying to figure life out. While that was definitely not an option for me in the midst of the locker room, it was the truth of where I was. But it was in this moment that I realized that there was nowhere to hide. I was either going forward or going back. God was using the sport of football to give me the courage to move forward in the game of life. Up until this point I had lived with so much fear, doubt, and unbelief that most of the time when it came to challenges, if I was not forced to go forward, I would simply stay where I was.

> **SPIRITUAL TRUTH**: *And Jesus answered them, 'Truly, I say to you, if you have faith and do not doubt, you will not only do what has been done to the fig tree, but even if you say to this mountain, 'Be taken up and thrown into the sea,' it will happen. (Matthew 21:21)*

But there was no staying in the locker room, because the little bit of faith I had inside of me was pushing me to go outside. I grabbed my helmet and shoulder pads and walked out into the muggy heat of the Jordan Matthews Jets practice field and began to prepare myself for what seemed would be a very tough day based on all the locker room chatter. Being a part of a team is one experience, but being a part of a football team is a total other journey. My heart was racing, and I felt so sick to my stomach. It was at this moment that Coach Senter said to all us, "Gentlemen I want to see a lot of heart today. You can't show or demonstrate fear, as it is the opposite of faith. My desire is for us all to be champions." I felt this amazing feeling of courage as Coach Senter spoke those words; they inspired me and quenched that feeling of doubt that I had in the pit of my stomach. I needed to hear those words for a number of reasons greater than playing the sport of football. As we prepared ourselves, Coach Senter brought us up as a team in a large huddle and said, "I want everyone to shout 'Champions' after the count of three." We all started to get pumped up as sweat poured off our facemasks, and we all shouted together, "Champions!!!"

As we did our individual drills, which were basically a time to sharpen the details of our positions, Coach Senter said to me, "You look good, Mason. You have quick feet like your brother Bucky." The one thing that I never considered was that my brother Bucky, who had played running back for Coach Senter, had set numerous records and was considered by many to have been a tremendous player. My brother had gone on to join the Marines, but people still talked about him, and I realized that I had some big shoes to fill.

It wasn't very long before I also realized that day that everyone expected me to be just as good as him. That is why I think Coach had desired for me to play the same position. He hoped I had the goods to be great, and I simply hoped that I could get through the day.

Then Coach Senter called my name. "Mason, get in at tailback." I ran into the huddle, nervous, sweating not from the heat, but from the pressure of actually playing. Coach called, "26 right toss on 1." I looked at Coach and with a quiet voice said, "Coach, that's the outside run, right?" He said, "Yes son, now make it happen." We broke the huddle, the QB snapped the ball and tossed it to me and off I ran for a score. I was floating as I ran back to the huddle, hoping to get another chance.

SPIRITUAL TRUTH: *I can do all things through Christ which strengthens me. (Philippians 4:13)*

After I made that one great play, my confidence grew and my memory of being this shy kid who lacked confidence had been forgotten, even if for a brief moment, I left the pain of my past and had an inner strength I had never felt before. I got back to the huddle and Coach Senter and my teammates said, "Great job." What a feeling of courage that gave me. Then Coach said, "I want this to be power play left, keep the ball inside and try to get as many yards as possible." We lined up again, the quarterback handed the ball off, and instead of taking the ball inside like Coach said, I decided to bounce the play outside.

It was at this moment I realized that in the sport of football and in the game of life, it is important to follow the instructions of those who understand how to play the game better than you. I tried to stay inside, but it seemed as though there was no hole to run in, so I just bounced the ball outside, thinking that I could do the same thing I did the play before. But this time there was a teammate named Vernon Harris who was right there ready to welcome me to varsity. As soon as I bounced that play outside, after Coach Senter had told me to keep the play inside, I got smashed. Vernon Harris hit me so hard that it lifted my feet off the ground. Everyone said, "Ooh," and I was like, "Ouch."

I wanted to quit as I picked myself up off the ground, and Coach Senter was there to meet me and say, "Are you okay, son?" I said, "Yes sir." In my mind that was it, I was done. I never wanted to experience another play like that. Getting knocked down on that play felt like all the other bad plays that had happened in my life. It made me feel like all the other tragedies I had experienced up until this point, like a failure. It was as if the things that had happened to my family and to me were my fault.

I had so many issues, but the only difference this time was that I had a coach and teammates who believed in me and who were right there to help me up and encourage me to keep going. In most cases in the past, every time something like this happened I always felt I had to give up. But this time God had put the right team of people around me and there was no stopping us. Coach Senter had set such a winning culture that quitting was not an option. He had set such a focus on pushing through the pain, and we had done so many physical and mental reps on it, that when I instinctively would have quit before, now my mind and body were doing something totally different. I could not believe it. I got up and threw the ball down, and sure, I wanted to quit, but something inside me would not all allow me to. Man, was I mad. How in the world had this happened to me? I told myself, "That will never happen to me again." I had had such a defeatist attitude so many times before, but this time I said "NO MORE." It took me getting knocked on my butt in a game called football to realize that life was not about quitting, giving up, or staying down, but about getting up when you have been knocked down and out. I was learning that no matter the circumstance or situation, the game of life will sometimes throw you, you have to get back up. God uses these moments to teach us that there will be good plays and bad plays, but we have to choose through it all if we are willing to play through adversity, regardless of the difficult times the game may present to us. I made the commitment that no matter how many times I may get knocked down, I was not out, and as long as I trust God, He will always give me the strength to get back up!

SPIRITUAL TRUTH: *Persecuted, but not abandoned; knocked down, but not destroyed. (2 Corinthians 4:9)*

CHAPTER 7

DOING THINGS THE RIGHT WAY

SPIRITUAL TRUTH: *There is a way that appears to be right, but in the end it leads to death. (Proverbs 14:12)*

There is always a way that seems right in the eyes and hearts of men. But then there comes that moment where you realize that what we are doing is not right. It takes having the right people with the right attitude to get us to this point. No matter how much we think we can do it on our own, God expects us to still look to him for guidance.

It was like any other typical summer, and my teammates and I were hanging out up at the Pantry parking lot. We did it every summer, just hanging out talking about cars, girls, and sports. No real in-depth conversation, just guys talking, and me a fifteen-year-old who was looking for a way to fit in. Although I had experienced more success than I ever could have imagined in the game of football, I was still struggling to make the right plays in the game of life. I personally and internally was still looking for my identity, hoping that somehow and in some way I could find complete confidence in something. Football gave me temporary moments of confidence from the small successes I would experience on the field of play, but as soon as I would return to the daily grind within the game of life, my insecurity, walls of mistrust, and pain would quickly return. I was searching for an answer, and any answer would do, as I wanted to feel affirmed, loved, and a part of something. Although football gave me some level of identity and confidence to at least not be such a loner, I still was not walking in freedom.

> **SPIRITUAL TRUTH**: *It is for freedom that Christ has set us free. Stand firm, then, and do not let yourselves be burdened again by a yoke of slavery. (Galatians 5:1)*

I wanted to be free of myself, but I simply did not know how to get free from this mental torment. Every day that passed in the game of life was another opportunity for the heart to become more hardened to the possibilities of God's complete work being established. This is when my good friend spoke up and said, "Hey fellas, I know we have been talking about cars, but down in Silk Hope is a garage where we can get some wheels." Oh, man. My mind started to race, and a big smile came upon my face. The smile came because although I knew what we were considering was wrong, I selfishly wanted those wheels at whatever cost. I did not care about the consequences, because for me it was about the quick emotional fix and satisfaction of having what I wanted temporally.

> **LIFE TRUTH**: *How many of us have made decisions based on the emotional effects within that brief moment in time, to ultimately make ourselves feel better, hoping that the feeling will last, only to realize later that it is gone?*

So my buddy said, "Are you guys down to go?" We all looked at each other, hoping that someone was going to say, "No, I am not down." But unfortunately that was not the case. One of the guys spoke up and said, "Of course we're down," as if to speak for the entire group. Collectively we let this one guy decide for all us to get into the car.

It was put up or shut up time; either be the one to chicken out, or be the one to get in the car and be affirmed by all my buddies. I really did not want to get in that car for a number of reasons, and the number one was my mother had already told me to be home before 11:30 pm. This discussion was taking place at 11:00 pm. I looked down at my watch as my mind raced, trying to decide if what I was doing was the right thing. Against my own conscience, I decided to get into that car, knowing it might be a big problem down the road. It was time to prove my toughness and desire to be part of the crew. I was seriously at a crossroad moment of sorts, left to make a game-time decision that deep down I knew was not going to be good. The feeling of being a part of something nullified all the fear I was feeling. I started to wrestle with the thought of my mom's voice saying, "Eddie, be home by 11:30 pm," but heard my buddy's voice saying, "Come on, man, let's go and see if we can get these rims. It won't take long."

LIFE TRUTH: *How many of us have been in that situation where we know the right thing to do, but we still choose to follow the wrong example? Where the rulebook is clear in order to provide a means of safety, a clear line of integrity to follow, but we allow for our emotions to prevail and crack under the peer pressure of pleasing others?*

It really came down to obedience and at this moment it was my opportunity to make a decision that was solely mine. I had followed so many others for so long, but the pride that had crept up in my heart caused me to lose my humility and the desire to choose what was wise. Sometimes that is all the game of life is about: choosing what is wise.

SPIRITUAL TRUTH: *How much better to get wisdom than gold, to get insight rather than silver! (Proverbs 16:16)*

My buddy's voice was speaking louder than my mom's wisdom and I decided to get inside the car. As we got inside the car I began to wrestle internally with the conviction of disobeying my mother and the feeling that something bad was going to happen. An internal beacon was flashing telling me, "Do not go." I would soon find out it would be one of the worst calls I had ever made. This was all because of the insecurities and anxieties that made me feel like I was not worthy. That's what fueled my poor choices, as really deep down I wanted people to like me, to feel important, and have some sense of value. But nothing was stopping me; I had made the decision. As we drove down the pitch-black country road with only the moon as our light, reality started to sink in: There was no turning back. The moment of truth was here. I could have stayed in the car and said, "You guys go ahead." But then I would be the chicken, the guy who was afraid and would not go all the way. I couldn't possibly let my teammates down, as they needed me. At least that is what I told myself. As my mother's voice of reason faded, my internal voice of foolishness got louder.

We parked on the side the road, got out of car, and started to walk up this road for what felt like an eternity. My buddies and I were going back and forth saying, "What kind of wheels are you going to get?" I said, "Man I am going to get me some spinners for my Volkswagen." I had worked very hard to earn the money to buy that Volkswagen. It was my pride and joy. I convinced myself at this moment that it was okay to steal, totally contrary to what my mother and grandparents had taught me all my life. As my grandfather had told me, there are two things that identify a man: His ability to keep his word and his ability to walk upright in integrity. I was breaking both. The wisdom that I should have cherished and taken to heart, I was despising.

> **SPIRITUAL TRUTH**: *The fear of the LORD is the beginning of knowledge, but fools despise wisdom and instruction. (Proverbs 1:7)*

As we got farther up the road, my buddy turned to me and said, "All we have to do is get over this fence and we are there."

I replied, "No, you guys go and we will wait here and watch out."

He said, "Okay, you guys be on the lookout and whistle if there is a problem." This was really my way of chickening out and making myself feel better, as I could always say that I did not cross the fence—I only stood by and watched.

Not soon after they had indeed crossed the fence, they returned with a few items that appeared to me to simply be junk. They were carrying five spinners and four hubcaps. I realized I had not made the right call; in fact, I was regretting getting in the car. I just wanted to go home and face my mom and the grounding she was going to give me for screwing up and making such a poor game-time decision. Right at that moment a flashlight came on and I heard a voice say, "Freeze! Put your hands up!" It didn't seem real, but the police were there and we all would soon learn that what had started as a simple journey down a road to get some wheels would turn into playing on a new field in the courtroom.

When I heard the policeman's voice, all I could do was run, the same way I had been running my whole life, from things that really were intended to make me face the truth of where I really was. This time however, there was no running as I was going to have to face the law, and the error of my mistakes. They did not catch me that night, because I ran out of fear into the woods and stayed there all night, hoping this ordeal I had put myself through would just go away, similar to how much of the pain of abuse and hurt I was living with would. I sat there in the woods that night freezing, with so many thoughts going through my head about my buddies, my mom, were we really in trouble, or was it a joke; I simply did not know what to think. All I knew is that whatever the case, I hoped it was not that serious.

Well, it turned out to be more serious than any of us could have expected, and in reality this bad judgment call made while everything was on the line in the game of life could have wound up costing me everything. But by God's grace it did not. God saw fit to work it out, but it did not come without leaving some scars in my mind and spirit that would intertwine and start to weave the character of who I really was. Although I wanted to change, make the right decisions, and do what was right, I simply did not know how. I personally needed to go through this trial in order for God to reveal who I was and what was really in my heart. Because up until this point, every game-time decision I had made was based on the appeal of man, never giving God a chance to prove and affirm who I really was in Him. It was my time to face the truth and start making the right call, but before I could do that I would have to win back the trust of my mom, coaches, teammates, and community. As in the game of life, the greatest game-time decision we have to make is the one that is in front of us that establishes us to be honest and trustworthy. Greater than the game of football I was learning to play, God was looking for me to learn how to make the right call in the game of life, to stop outside the borders and gates of the field of pain I had been accustomed to playing on and to start to truly identify myself as a player who could be trusted in football, but more importantly, in the game of life.

> **SPIRITUAL TRUTH**: *Furthermore, you shall select out of all the people able men who fear God, men of truth, those who hate dishonest gain; and you shall place these over them as leaders of thousands, of hundreds, of fifties and of tens. (Exodus 18:21)*

CHAPTER 8

LEARNING TO BE FAITHFUL

TRUTH FINALLY was staring me in the face, and it was unavoidable. I had to finally be that man who looked himself in the mirror. It really was no different from when Coach Senter had told us so many times to run a play this way, but we continued to try to run the play we thought would work, only to realize in the end that his experience, knowledge, and wisdom was greater than our speed and talent. The only problem in this situation was it wasn't just about running a football play in the right gap or not. I was dealing with some serious personal issues, and one was learning to be faithful.

> **SPIRITUAL TRUTH:** *"Whoever can be trusted with very little can also be trusted with much, and whoever is dishonest with very little will also be dishonest with much. (Luke 16:10)*

I had not been very faithful up to this point, especially when it came to dealing with truth and honesty with myself and who I really was. Ultimately, this is half the battle when it comes to the game of life: truly owning who you are as a person. Football had created one identity of who people saw me to be, but it really was not who I was. I was still this little boy who had been hurt from the pain of abuse and who had seen up close and personal what anger can do to a marriage. I had struggled with finding the identity of who I really was, and I still cried out to be affirmed by others. Understanding and facing who I was would prove to be my greatest battle. Not to mention the fact that I still had to win back the trust of my mother, grandparents, teachers, friends, and coaches. That had become my main focus.

SPIRITUAL TRUTH: *Commit your way to the LORD; trust in him and he will do this. (Psalm 37:5)*

The shame of going to school the weekend after the wheel incident was so hard. I wanted to hide from the idea of what people might think of me, or how they would judge me. I felt so alone, but I knew I had no choice but to get up, dust myself off, and go, but not until after my mom and I had an extensive conversation about the whole matter.

Her first question was, "Why did you do it son, why didn't you just come home like I told you?"

I responded, "Mom, I just wanted to be like one of the boys and feel a part of the crew."

But then she adamantly responded, "Eddie, how many times have I told you that God created you to be your own man and to follow no one? To blaze your own trail and let others follow the good works of your own life?"

I had no response as I hung my head in shame, knowing that I had disappointed my mother. She said, "Son, you will recover from this and God will do all the great things you are willing to expect Him to do. But you can't doubt in your heart." It gave me a sense of hope, which in most cases is all you need to take the next step toward true change. She said, "Get up, dust yourself off, and face the truth." These words, although simple in nature, were prophetic in spirit, because that is exactly what I needed to do.

> **SPIRITUAL TRUTH:** *as the secrets of their hearts are laid bare. So they will fall down and worship God, exclaiming, 'God is really among you!' (1 Corinthians 14:25)*

I walked into the school expecting a bunch of whispers and people pointing fingers, but that is not how it was. Coach Senter, Coach Phillips, and Coach Wadford were right there with open arms to let me know they had my back and that this was just carelessness, foolishness, and bad decision-making by a group of young men trying to find their way. It was as if God had revealed my heart to them, to know that the game film of my life was in no way indicative of who I was as a person. This really fueled my passion to right the wrong that I had done and start truly taking the severity of my actions seriously.

My goal was to figure out what would be the best way to prove to God, the people I hurt, and myself that I did not mean to do this. But like most people, I wanted my mistakes to go away as quickly as they happened. This is never the case, as there is a learning process We must go through in order to get the lesson that the Lord is trying to teach us directly. I just wanted to say, "I'm sorry, please forgive me and let me get my life together."

I am reminded of some of football meetings I've been in, when the coach is getting on my butt to improve my game so that I can be the best player I can. That is exactly what God has to take us through. He needed for me to get the lesson and value that comes in not only saying "I'm sorry," but taking that "sorry" and turning it from pain into a direct purpose to be used for God's glory. Faithfulness to change would take a direct connection to be open to doing things a new way. To be quite honest, it was a lesson I was very familiar with from my coach. If we were running a play that did not work, he would change the play based on his experience and wisdom to find the right play that would eventually work. God essentially was using my mom, my coaches, and my grandparents to give me a new set of plays and downs that would motivate me to become more faithful and obedient and to follow after the wisdom and instruction that would lead me down the right path in the game of life.

CHAPTER 9

THE RIGHT VOICE

WHEN YOU ARE SEARCHING for yourself, have made major mistakes, and are still recovering and sorting out how to deal with life as it has played out before you, committing to turning over a new leaf can be very difficult. At best, we can find ourselves looking for people who meet wants over our needs. This means that they only tell us what we want to hear, not what we need to hear. We expose ourselves to the persuasive words of unsound judgment instead of relying on the spiritual power that rests in God to play out the game of life His way.

> **SPIRITUAL TRUTH:** *When I came to you, brothers, I did not come with eloquence or superior wisdom as I proclaimed to you the testimony about God. For I resolved to know nothing while I was with you except Jesus Christ and him crucified. I came to you*

in weakness and fear, and with much trembling. My message and my preaching were not with wise and persuasive words, but with a demonstration of the Spirit's power, so that your faith might not rest on men's wisdom, but on God's power. (1 Corinthians 2:1–5)

Even though we are taught not to rely on men's words, we still need people who have decided to be great examples for God to help show us a new way of dealing with life's issues. We cannot just assume we will still know what to do without having others help us create game-time momentum that will start to give us the success we are looking for, which is why we cannot just allow anybody to be a part of our team in the game of life. If we truly want to win in the game of life, we really have to look at whom we are playing the game with. We don't just want anybody—we want the right people who are called to our lives to encourage us in the process of our healing. Most of the time these people come in many forms at key moments in our lives to help us make real-time, game-changing decisions.

The reason we need these game-changing mentors is because they coach us out of a defeatist attitude in moments of life where we have lost and into believing that we can win. They help us see the game of life as winnable, even when defeat appears inevitable. They have a way of seeing life as an open door of opportunity regardless of what the last play in the game has presented to us. They help us own our mistakes, but minimize their effects on our mindsets which may affect the outcome of the present play that we have right in front of us. For most of us the greatest battles we experience are the ones that are taking place in our minds. Unfortunately for me, there was a real war going on inside my head that made me struggle with my identity and with pulling myself out of this mental mess. In sports they call it being in a mental funk. It is when no matter what people say to you, nothing seems to work. I seriously could not grasp the concept that mistakes happen to every one, and that some of our greatest lessons come from the mistakes we make. Not that it is the best way to learn, but it definitely gives us something to learn from, mature in, and change into. My personal confidence was shot, my faith had been shaken, and I really did not feel worthy of forgiveness because I felt that I had let everyone down.

SPIRITUAL TRUTH: *Finally, brethren, whatsoever things are true, whatsoever things [are] honest, whatsoever things [are] just, whatsoever things [are] pure, whatsoever things [are] lovely, whatsoever things [are] of good report; if [there be] any virtue, and if [there be] any praise, think on these things. (Philippians 4:8)*

Although I wanted to think differently and start winning in the game of life on a personal, spiritual, mental, physical, and emotional level, I had lost my confidence and my ability to believe and developed anxiety because my mistake was not private but public. Coaches Senter, Wadford, and Phillips tried their best during my sophomore year, but I was struggling emotionally. Although my grades, my game, and my life as a whole was affected by the last game time decision, God was not going to allow the company I was keeping to affect me anymore.

LIFE TRUTH: *Isn't it amazing how misery loves company?*

I was at a place where the majority of my problem was the company I had chosen to keep. Every time we had a break from the class, I gravitated right to the crowd that continued to reiterate the poor decision we had made on that night. We would stand there saying, "Man what do you think the judge will decide about our fate? Do you think we will get off?" Going on and on, over and over that last play, instead of recognizing that there was nothing any of us involved could do.

SPIRITUAL TRUTH: *Therefore, take up the full armor of God, so that you will be able to resist in the evil day, and having done everything, to stand firm. Stand firm therefore. (Ephesians 6:13)*

It was time to start listening to a new set of voices and keeping company that would encourage me out of my mess and not keep me in it. Just as I did in my freshmen year when I got knocked down, I had to get back up and press forward. That is exactly what happened in one of our high school football games. Coach had put me in at running back, knowing that my mind, spirit, confidence, and heart were still shaken from all that was going on. For whatever reason, he looked past my faults and forced me to continue to take on the game of life, regardless of what the outcome looked like.

Coach came to me and called the very same play he had called over a year ago, "26 Toss right." But this time it would be a different outcome; instead of taking it to the house, I got hammered by the defense. I ran to the sideline of life, like many of us do when we get knocked down, hoping that the coach would take me out of the game. But instead, he looked me right in my eyes and yelled at me and said, "Are you ready now son! Get your butt up, get in there, and score!" It took another big hit and my coach's voice to speak life back into me to believe that I could win, and not only win, but win big in the game of life. It was as if God led Coach Senter to tell me, "You are going to get knocked down in life, but it is how you respond after you get knocked down that matters! Get back up, son." I yelled to myself and to my teammates, "Let's go!" The fire and burning desire came back as I jogged back onto the field from the sideline, but as I was running Coach Senter called me and said, "Eddie, you ready now?"

I was overcome with emotion on the inside and started tearing up with passion. I had this burning desire to go in there to run for my life. I sprinted back onto the field and coach called the same play, 26 Toss Right, which is a run play to the right side. That is really what God does; He places us in the same challenging situation a second time to see if we will respond differently. The only difference is, because I actually took Coach Senter's words to heart this time, I knew I was going to score. In fact, before the play happened, I told myself, "You are going to score."

We snapped the ball, and our quarterback handed me the ball and off I went, sixty-five yards to pay dirt. That feeling of knowing I could win, have victory, and not walk in the shadows of defeat anymore reestablished my confidence to believe I could. It was the one play I needed in order to realize that although the game of life can present some pretty tough obstacles, sometimes the thing that we need in order to get back up is to get knocked back down but depend on God's power and not our own. To trust in the words and right voices that are there to encourage us, and not discourage us. It is in these intimate moments of weakness that God demonstrates his Mighty Right Hand. He shows us His loving grace and unmerited favor and causes us to gain confidence and not be afraid to go into the game of life. He knows that although there will be ups and downs, we still have a responsibility to play, and not just play, but play hard. We know that He has not called us to walk in the shadows of defeat, but to experience Victory that comes from being in His presence and depending on His power. The only major call we have to make is which voice is going to be more powerful: the one in our head, or the one that God is trying to establish in our heart. You make the call.

CHAPTER 10

OWNING YOUR MISTAKES

AS YOU MIGHT IMAGINE, the trouble I had gotten into did not come without punishment. Although I had gotten over my issues of insecurity and beating myself up, I still had to own up to the responsibilities of dealing with the consequences of my mistake. Although it is a biblical truth to forget the former things, it is very important that we not forget our mistakes prior to taking responsibility for them, so we actually get the lesson that God is trying to teach us.

> **SPIRITUAL TRUTH:** *All Scripture is inspired by God and is useful to teach us what is true and to make us realize what is wrong in our lives. It corrects us when we are wrong and teaches us to do what is right. God uses it to prepare and equip his people to do every good work. (2 Timothy 3:16–17)*

I had hoped to simply make it disappear in my mind, and although my way worked well as a temporary fix, it would not as a long-term solution. As I had learned so many times from playing football, when Coach Senter was trying to get you to change something about your game, he would address the direct issue that was causing the problem in the first place. To avoid what needed to be corrected is to miss the greater good in the lesson in the game of life that God was trying to show to me. So the Lord used this circumstance to teach me the value of not running away from my problems, but to confront them head on and take ownership of not just what I had done, but also how to play a role in mending what may have been broken. When it comes to the problems that we oftentimes deal with, it is better to understand the power that lives in perfecting winning the small, game-time battles that are in front of us, instead of trying to simply win the game. To not take the game of life head on with focused intent to win the good and bad plays that happen in each game-time moment and decision that has to be made is to avoid and ignore the ones that need to be corrected. God never intended for us to play the game of life, hoping that the mistakes we are making will fix themselves on their own. Rather, His expectation is to not only win, but to win with the right mindset, ridding ourselves of anything that is hindering our progress.

SPIRITUAL TRUTH: *You were running the race so well. Who has held you back from following the truth? (Galatians 5:7)*

God does his greatest work on us when He takes us into the meeting room of life, makes us address what is hindering us, gives us the corrections we need to make, and then helps us take responsibility for the mistakes we have made by righting the wrong that has been done. It was my time to take ownership for that night I had gotten into trouble, but shame and embarrassment were trying to resurface as the opponents that had tackled me so many times before. I needed a victory over the emotional tug I felt in my heart, and as God always does, He takes a mess and turns it into a miracle. But it does not always look like what we think it should.

Even though I had gotten into this trouble, God had delivered me and given me 400 hours of community service as a means to teach me the lesson I needed to learn. I had to decide between the option of working at a community center or the police station, and I chose the police station. I had wanted to be a police officer as long as I could remember. I already had a healthy respect for authority, but I was like any other sixteen-year-old boy, still trying to figure life out, using my mistakes as a means of learning instead of just adhering to the wisdom of people like Coaches Phillips and Senter, Mom, and Grandpa. Although from an outward appearance it looked like I had no respect for authority, my Grandpa had raised me to respect authority. My biggest issue was that I did not respect myself or trust my own judgment, so I depended on that of others.

> **SPIRITUAL TRUTH**: *Let your roots grow down into him, and let your lives be built on him. Then your faith will grow strong in the truth you were taught, and you will overflow with thankfulness. (Colossians 2:7)*

But it was my time to stop relying on the decisions of others and start taking responsibility and serving my community. It was time to let all that I had been taught shine through at key moments in my life, when it appeared everything was on the line.

So my grandfather took me to my first day of community service, and I have to be honest, I was nervous because I really did not know what to expect. Even though I had gained my confidence back, I was ashamed of the memory of when I was arrested. The last time I was at the police station, my mom was turning me in and I was getting handcuffs taken off and being sent to have my fingerprints taken.

So many negative memories popped into my head as we walked in. One of the first things I saw was the jail cell they had locked me up in, and I was taken right back to that moment of when I was arrested for the incident that night when I was hanging out with my friends. My grandfather told Captain Fox, who had been my Little League football coach, "He's in your hands," as if to send a message of agreement that was intent on bringing about positive change in my heart.

Captain Fox said, "I got him, Mr. Cheek." They looked at each other as only two men could and had in mind that they were determined to turn my life around and in the process teach me the lessons I needed to know to get me to the next level. I was learning the value of how important it is to have father figures in this game we call life, learning that every young man needs a father figure, someone to look up to in times of need, times when you need a word of wisdom and an anchor.

My day at the police station started with cleaning the bathrooms, sweeping, and emptying trashcans in the unit. They did not compromise on doing the little things. It felt a lot like being at Coach Senter's practice. The only difference was the pressure to perform was a lot higher than being on the football field. Knowing that I was not there on my own accord but that my presence was court-ordered and mandated community service, I had no choice but to do everything I was told. I could have skipped football practice and the worst I would have had to do is run some sprints or sit out a game. But if I messed this up, I was going to jail.

That was the exact amount of pressure I needed to bring out the best in me. I was finally realizing that I had played the game of life the wrong way for so long that I really did not know how to play it right. As I performed the work expected of me, the officers would occasionally say to me, "Don't forget to ensure that you do things right, as to not break your probation." They were not saying it to remind me of my mistake, but rather to focus on the importance of doing the little things right.

I was terrified of making a mistake, because although I had made a mistake that sent me there, at the core of who I was I was a good kid. There was a part of me that did not like doing the community service, but every time that thought came, I would cast it down and refocus on the tasks at hand, as I wanted it to be over the very day it started. Not because I did not like it, but because I was embarrassed. As I was washing the police cars, people would drive by and honk, making me think they were making fun of me. Although deep down I was embarrassed, I had my mind made up not to make the same mistakes again. Instead I focused on taking each task seriously, as they gave it to me.

It seemed like they had so many cars to wash, and they were all filthy. Now this may have been my mind just angry at the fact that this was the first time that I had to do something where I had no choice because the consequences were so high. But this is really how God wants us to play the game of life. He wants us to take it seriously and to realize if we don't, it can cost us.

SPIRITUAL TRUTH: *Suppose one of you wants to build a tower. Won't you first sit down and estimate* *the cost to see if you have enough money to complete it? In the same way, those of you who do not give up everything you have cannot be my disciples. (Luke 14:28)*

When it comes to playing out the game of life, we all must weigh the cost of our mistakes and make a serious decision that is committed to long-term change. We have to see beyond what we are doing and instead focus on how what we are doing will affect the greater good that God desires to establish in the game of life. I was learning that, as a I sweated and cleaned those cars that day.

SPIRITUAL TRUTH: *The LORD detests all the proud of heart. Be sure of this: They will not go unpunished. (Proverbs 16:5)*

The first day had been so long from cleaning the building and the cars that I started to whine internally and mentally. The longer the day went on, the more I wanted to leave and start making things about me. The commitment I had started with to do things their way was starting to fade. I just wanted out, to leave, but there was no leaving. I never even considered that this was the same prideful attitude that had gotten me in trouble in the first place. That pride was trying to come back into my heart and the lesson I thought I had learned had not really taken hold at all.

The officers at the station came out to check on my work, and one officer said, "Son, come here." By the tone of his voice as he inspected the cars, I could tell he was not pleased at all. I had this big lump in my throat as I waited for him to scold me. He said again, "Come here." I was so hesitant, because it felt like when my dad used to discipline me. I simply was overcome with fear. My thought process was, I got in trouble, got reprimanded and disciplined for it, was serving my probation and community service, and now I was carrying out the responsibilities of my probation and community service. But that was all extrinsic. Everything for me was focused on how it looked to man, not to God.

All I was concerned with was the act of doing, not the act of changing. True change is a process, and the process is never ending. In reality my process had just started and I simply did not know that. Because as I washed those cars, the one thing they told me was, "After every car, please come and get one of the deputies to approve your work." I was only half-listening, so I heard, "Come and get one of the deputies." I did not hear "After every car." Had I listened I would have had it a whole lot easier first day. To be honest, that is the greater lesson in it all. God truly desires for us to get the simple lesson of listening to the wisdom of those who are already more experienced in playing the game of life, so we can do greater works for His glory.

SPIRITUAL TRUTH: *But God chose the foolish things of the world to shame the wise; God chose the weak things of the world to shame the strong. (1 Corinthians 1:27)*

Although I had in some way washed those cars with a smile on my face, I forgot the power in the lesson of simply listening to the details. That lesson continued to play out over and over; it was the same one that, had I listened to my mom, would have saved me from all the trouble I was in. Her words, "Be home by 11:30 pm," echoed to me again. How could I have forgotten to listen? I could have saved myself so much time and work. But here I was again, having to start over and redo a task over again. This is the power of sin.

SPIRITUAL TRUTH: *So let us stop going over the basic teachings about Christ again and again. Let us go on instead and become mature in our understanding. Surely we don't need to start again with the fundamental importance of repenting from evil deeds and placing our faith in God. (Hebrews 6:1)*

God Himself declares this as a standard and will not compromise it in His word. When someone is trying to coach you out of your mess, don't compromise those instructions.

SPIRITUAL TRUTH: *My sheep listen to my voice; I know them, and they follow me. (John 10:27)*

This is so critical when it comes to being successful. I had no idea that washing those cars and then having to rewash them would teach me so many lessons for the game of life. Never did I imagine on that one day that the lessons would stick with me as a young man, teaching me day by day, as I finished up my community service, to embrace the power of owning my mistakes instead of trying to hide behind them and reject them. God was preparing me for greatness in the game of life.

What examples of instruction in your life can you remember that you are still practicing today? Have you been consistent and committed to practicing these life lessons on a daily basis?

CHAPTER 11

GOD'S GRACE

ONE THING we never want to take for granted in the game of life is God's grace. Grace gives us a right perspective and appreciation of God and all that He has given us, regardless of what circumstance or opposition we may be facing in the game of life.

> **SPIRITUAL TRUTH:** *But he said to me, 'My grace is sufficient for you, for my power is made perfect in weakness.' Therefore I will boast all the more gladly about my weaknesses, so that Christ's power may rest on me. (2 Corinthians 12:9)*

Now when it comes to grace, the biggest opponent we will face is the battle between what we can do versus what God can. Grace truly does help us realize that we are really not that good. It helps us to understand that without it we cannot do anything, which is the very reason He allows for us to go through certain circumstances to gain a greater appreciation of His grace. To help us become more dependent on Him, instead of ourselves. There is nothing better than experiencing the power that lives within God's grace as He pours it out to heal the hurt of disappointments that we experience, so we know that He is always there, regardless of what we face.

Life was pretty good at this point: I had four scholarship opportunities from Division 1 universities. I was still recovering from the shame of that trouble I had gotten in, but time had passed and I had learned to work myself out of some of those situations, through the probation, lessons I had learned, and just really willing myself. That was the problem—I had set in my mind that I was doing it, forgetting that it was by God's grace that the opportunities were right in front of me. Because to be honest, although I was good at the sport of football, my track record was not that good at playing the game of life. I was still a selfish kid who was trying to find his way and who had learned more how to manage the game of life instead of playing it the right way. People were giving me all the wisdom and lessons on how to play it the right way, but my pride was just not allowing me to apply what I was learning.

It was like any other morning. I was joking with my buddies as we were walking into the main entrance of the school, pushing and shoving one another, talking about what we had to do that day. I was on a high from a lot of the great things that were happening in my life, really for the first time in a long time. I had not gotten into any trouble and things were starting to line up, but as I entered the school my guidance counselor stopped me and said, "Eddie, we need to talk."

I responded, "About what?"

"Your transcript. It appears that you do not have enough credits for admissions to the colleges that are recruiting you."

"What do you mean? I have all my credits."

She said, "Unfortunately, Eddie, you don't."

The reality of facing the truth sometimes can be so hard that it forces things we thought we had overcome to resurface. I started to get agitated and a little bit angry, as I was looking for answers as to how this could happen. I asked, "How did this happen, what did I do wrong, how did this get missed?" In my heart what I was saying is, "How did you let this happen?"

She had no answer except, "Eddie, it was just an oversight and the only thing you can do is take a summer credit." Here we go, another roadblock. My heart sank. My first thought was, not again. Why does my bubble of hope continue to get burst? Why, why? I was angry and wanted this to be a mistake, but it wasn't, and the more it became a reality the more I became discouraged. All the discouragement was because I had learned to expect bad things to happen. Even when good was present, I could not recognize it. Really what I was doing and practicing in the game of life was devaluing God's grace and the greater good that was before me. I was focused more on empowering the bad that was happening, instead of finding the good.

She said, "Eddie, I know you have been through a lot and this is hard, but you are so close. You can't turn back now."

The voices of all those who had encouraged me started to play out in my head, and for the first time in my life I did not allow for this to stress me out. I wanted to throw in the towel and sink my shoulders, but this time I rolled them back and asked her, "What do I have to do?" I was not going to give myself an option of losing in the game of life when I had learned how to win in the game of football. I made a mental commitment that I was not going to allow this bump in the road to get in the way of my dream.

She told me, "You have to take one science credit, and you will have to take it at a local community college. The only problem is that you cannot do it until this summer." My back was against the wall, as I had done everything right academically, but had an oversight on my transcript for this one credit. Failure was not an option and I was not going to be defeated.

SPIRITUAL TRUTH: *For the Lord your God is he who goes with you to fight for you against your enemies, to give you the victory. (Deuteronomy 20:4)*

I was in the game of my life and everything was on the line. So many great things were in front of me, but so many bad things were with me. My coach and I immediately got on the phone with the college recruiters, and many of them pulled the scholarship offers within days once they understood the issue. But one school did not. They stuck by me and committed to their offer. Coach Moody demonstrated that the man whom I met and felt was sincere really was. He showed me that he believed in me as a person, not just a football player. God was giving me such a real moment of grace that it blew my mind, especially after all the disappointment I had experienced from all the schools telling me no. But for every no that I received, by God's grace He had given me the ultimate yes. What a feeling to know that when it seems like nothing is going right, God still believes in us. This is exactly what grace does; it takes that which seems impossible and injects faith into our hope to help us believe that all things are possible.

SPIRITUAL TRUTH: *You who are trying to be justified by the law have been alienated from Christ; you have fallen away from grace. (Galatians 5:4)*

But when we are faced with the reality of what I was facing, it is really hard to receive God's grace. We can become so focused on the emotional, spiritual, and sometimes physical opposition that it blinds us to the unmerited favor and grace that God is trying to pour out into our lives. This is exactly how I had learned to live and play the game of life: By a set of rules and regulations that were totally contrary to the word of God. I had become so reliant on my own ability that it never allowed for God's Grace to come in and provide His strength even in my frail weakness.

The true blessing and grace was the fact that I still had a scholarship offer on the table. That was God's sovereign grace. The whole intent was to cause me to rely on God, instead of myself. But how hard is that? When your back is against the wall, you are no longer in control of the situation. You have experienced so many letdowns and really don't have the faith to know that the outcome of the game of life will be won, not based on your power, but in His. That is exactly where I was.

When my counselor told me, "Eddie, you have missed one credit," that wasn't a big deal. But when the one credit caused those whom I thought had my back and believed in me to give up on me, I was shaken. Besides, I really did not have any other options; I was out of plays on what to call in the game of life. I thought, "What am I to do? How will I get out of this situation?" I could easily work hard right; but I had one school left and really was not sure what would be the outcome.

When I received the call, I was sitting in my classroom. Through the intercom system, I heard, "Eddie, please come up to Coach Senter's office." It was one of the longest walks I have ever had to take, knowing that there was going to be some news delivered that would either launch me into destiny or destroy it. I was nervous, but when I got there, I could overhear Coach Senter on the phone with someone, and as I entered his office somewhat shaken, he said, "Eddie, have a seat, Coach Moody wants to speak with you." I grabbed the phone, expecting that he was going to tell me the same thing the other three schools had told me: "We are not going to be offering you a scholarship."

But that is not even close to what he said. First, he told me that he was extremely proud of me and of the hard work I had put in to get to this point. He said, "We have been monitoring your success both on and off the field, and it is very apparent that you are the type of human being we want at our university. You have shown us that once you set a goal, you will complete it, regardless of what it takes. This is exactly what Coach Brown and I believe will help us win not only today, but in the future. So we want you to know we are sticking with you and will hold our offer of scholarship for you until you finish your summer course. When you are ready, you will be given the opportunity of having a full scholarship to the University of North Carolina."

I could not believe it. My mind was blown. How and why me? Why would they choose me? So many other people had given up on me, why not you guys? So many questions were in my mind, causing me to question all the what-ifs and negatives that were happening, that I never even thought that this was God's glorious grace, and yet in that brief moment I was blinded by the pain of the past experiences that had occurred in the game of life.

We all have done it—been guilty of missing God's grace because we become so focused on what is wrong that we can't even see what is right. But then there was this moment when Coach Moody said again, "Eddie, we are excited and we want you."

I asked, "Coach, are you serious?"

He said, "Yes, we are serious." I leaped out of my seat as if I had just won the state championship, so overcome with joy that I started to cry. I said, "Thank you coach, thank you for believing in me!" This is the full intent of God's Grace, to produce joy unspeakable in our hearts that births a winning attitude in our minds. I said, "Coach, thank you, thank you, and thank you!" He said, "Finish strong son, finish strong and we will be in touch!"

Coach Senter hugged my neck and said, "Very proud of you, Eddie, now get back to class!" I was floating when I left his office. Even though I still felt disappointed about losing the other three scholarship opportunities, I still was encouraged that I had the opportunity for one.

SPIRITUAL TRUTH: *And David inquired at the LORD, saying, Shall I pursue after this troop? shall I overtake them? And he answered him, Pursue: for* *thou shalt surely overtake them, and without fail recover all. "...But David encouraged himself in the Lord" (1 Samuel 30:6)*

That is exactly what I had to do: Not allow for what I lost to overshadow the grace of God that I had gained in the one scholarship. Hearing the words from both Coaches Moody and Senter encouraged me in the greater game of life that was playing out before me. It definitely was not easy, but I soon realized that as long as I kept a heart of appreciation for what I did have, instead of what I didn't have, God's grace would always shine through and the Lord would be glorified.

The key in this moment is for all to realize that good and bad happen to us in the game of life. But our perspective is what will help us keep a winning attitude in the game of life as it plays out before us. If we don't keep that winning attitude, we risk losing the greatest gift that gives us a winning position in the game of life, which is ultimately His Grace!

CHAPTER 12

PRIORITIES IN LIFE

AFTER MY FIRST few workouts my body, mind, and spirit had started to adjust to the rigors of university life. In fact, as the first semester rolled along, I started to skip classes and forget all the words that Coach Brown originally had spoken to us. I was getting a little too comfortable with the environment and had started to figure out ways to take shortcuts. We had started training camp for football, had all our strength and conditioning tests, and practices were becoming routine. I was starting to settle in to college life, which is normally the time, whether in life or sports, that we start to make the most mistakes, as pride begins to take over as we experience more and more success. When we should be working harder to keep what God has placed in our hands, instead we start to devalue the opportunities and treat them as though we deserve it, instead of continuing to earn it.

SPIRITUAL TRUTH: *then your heart will become proud and you will forget the LORD your God who brought you out from the land of Egypt, out of the house of slavery. (Deuteronomy 8:14)*

To be honest, this was not something that had started overnight, but over time. I had been an excellent high school student, simply because my mother demanded the best, and would not allow me to compromise my academics. But mom was not here on a daily basis to yell at me, so I made every excuse as to why I started to experience failure, from blaming it on my friends, to classes were too hard, to practices were too long, to whatever I could find. The one big mistake I was making in the game of life was devaluing and dismissing the relationships of those who had been so integral in helping me overcome many of my struggles. It was not intentional, but it was exactly what the enemy wants to do to all of us—get us comfortable during periods of life transitions, when it appears we are winning on the outside, but on the inside we are really losing. When we need to be focusing on building greater relationships that can be of greater benefit to hold us accountable, we instead wind up allowing other distractions in life to get us off course of where God really wants us to be.

SPIRITUAL TRUTH: *And this I speak for your own profit; not that I may cast a snare upon you, but for that which is comely, and that ye may attend upon the Lord without distraction. (1 Corinthians 7:35)*

This is exactly what had started to occur. As I said earlier, it wasn't like this behavior had just started; it was something I had practiced for many years. I would go for a period of time doing things well, but because I had not made up in my mind about who and what was most important in my life, I would simply get distracted. This can happen to anyone who has not chosen to have God as the central figure and guiding force for every play that we make in the game of life. When we have not made this commitment, we can rest assured that our priorities in life can become an issue. I did not even notice what was happening, as it had all been communicated to us from day one. Our academic advisor had warned us of all the do's and don'ts of campus life. He had told us about all the campus parties, the ladies, the hangouts, the fraternities, and so much more that could easily cause us to lose focus on what was most important: our academics.

SPIRITUAL TRUTH: *He whose ear listens to the life-giving reproof will dwell among the wise. He who neglects discipline despises himself, but he who listens to* *reproof acquires understanding. The fear of the LORD is the instruction for wisdom, and before honor comes humility. (Proverbs 15: 31–33)*

It was very clear from our first meeting with Brian Davis, his staff, and the coaches at UNC that academics and graduating from the university were of utmost importance. The standard had been set, and all of us freshmen knew it. But man, the parties, ladies, and hangouts seemed be so much more fun. Having no one to answer to or tell me I had to be in by 11 pm made me rely on the foolishness that was in my heart. I never realized that these distractions would take me down a road to destruction. It is amazing how you don't even notice the destruction and devastation within the power of distraction until it is too late.

Midterms came and we had our first academic check-in with Brian Davis. We didn't realize the magnitude of the situation until Brain called fifteen of us freshman into his office. What I thought would be a meeting of encouragement and check-in became a real reality check for me. I thought to my-self, "They care so much about us," never realizing that this meeting was placing us all on academic probation. Academics had become so easy for me that I had assumed that the same study habits I had in high school would be enough to get me through college. That was not even close to the case, because for every level God raises us up, so does the standard. God had raised me to a level spiritually, emotionally, and physically, but I thought what I was doing was enough. Although success can be your greatest asset in the game of life, it can also become your greatest liability if not respected.

I had to find this out the hard way when we were called into the meeting with our academic advisor. From his tone as we all walked into the meeting, I could tell it was serious. Brian said, "Men, this meeting is to address the fact that the University of North Carolina has placed you all on academic probation for not adhering to the standard that has been set. You are currently ineligible to play because of your inability to attend class and finish the necessary course load that has been requested of you. If you do not raise your grades prior to the end of this semester you will not be eligible to compete in spring ball next semester."

I thought to myself, "Oh my God, my mom is going to kill me. How in the world did I get here?" A great question, but a foolish one. I knew exactly how I had arrived at this place: By losing my focus on the integrity of who I was and who God had called me to be. I was more interested in partying, chasing girls, hanging out, and drinking instead of fulfilling my responsibilities on and off the field. I asked Brian, "What's the next step?"

He said, "You will attend mandatory study hall, do extra

work, and pass all exams that you have left. It's that simple, because there really are no other options." This felt so much like the night I had gotten into trouble in high school, when I knew the right thing to do but had still chosen to do the wrong thing. I knew the plays in the game of life were not working, but I still chose to use them because they were convenient and because of my inability to be responsible, respect authority, and do what I was supposed to do.

> **SPIRITUAL TRUTH:** *If anyone, then, knows the good they ought to do and doesn't do it, it is sin for them. (James 4:17)*

It is very simple in the eyes of God. When we choose to not do what we are supposed to do in the game of life, it is sin. We can make all kinds of excuses as to why we find ourselves in bad situations in life, but much of the reason why is that we have chosen not to run the plays that God has designed for us to run, using integrity and fulfilling the prioritized obligations that God has called us to. God expects us to place a priority on doing what is right, as there will always be someone or something that will come to distract you from who and what God has called you to be. We cannot live our lives based on what feels right, but what is right.

CHAPTER 13

THE CONSEQUENCES THAT LIVE IN OUR CHOICES

IT WAS TIME for me to focus and start to work my way out of this hole I had dug for myself. The crazy thing is that as much as I was gaining focus in one area of my life, I was losing it in another. Every time something bad happened in my life, I had a history of giving in to things that made me feel good about myself.

> **SPIRITUAL TRUTH:** *For those who live according to the flesh set their minds on the things of the flesh, but those who live according to the Spirit set their minds on the things of the Spirit. (Romans 8:5)*

Just when I was about to take two steps forward in the game of life, I wind up taking four steps backwards. It was all simply a lack of self-esteem and confidence that seemed to choke the life out of the possibilities of greatness that God placed inside of me. At this stage of my life, two things made me feel good. First, I really wanted people to like me, so I tried my best to be the "life of the party." Second, I had always struggled with being affirmed by other people because of the bad experiences I had gone through in the first quarter of my life. I was also still feeling my father's rejection. Although it was not a physical thing at this point in my life, it was etched in the back of mind the same way as one of the worst plays I had made that may have cost me the game. I wanted someone to love me and to help me feel good about where I was in life. To make me feel like I was better than where I really was. I had relied on my coaches, mom, and grandparents for so long that when they were not there I really started to look for love in the wrong places.

I adored my girlfriend, and although I did not know how to give love, I surely knew how to receive it. She made me feel good about myself when I was down, and my way of expressing my feelings to her was through sex. I never took into account the consequences having sex before marriage would lead to, as well as never being fully committed to the process that God had me in. I wanted to tell her how I felt but did not know how to because of my immaturity, selfishness, and inability to understand and connect with my emotions because of the pain from my past. Major insecurities existed in my life because of the abuse I had witnessed, and these insecurities caused me to cross boundaries and commit sin that led to a very serious situation in both of our lives. Because we had chosen a life of immorality, we compromised our core values and used sex as a justification to live immorally. I made up every excuse as to why it was the right thing to do because of how it made me feel.

> **SPIRITUAL TRUTH:** *But I say, walk by the Spirit, and you will not gratify the desires of the flesh. For the desires of the flesh are against the Spirit, and the desires of the Spirit are against the flesh, for these are opposed to each other, to keep you from doing the things you want to do. But if you are led by the Spirit, you are not under the law. Now the works of the flesh are evident: sexual immorality, impurity, sensuality, idolatry, sorcery, enmity, strife, jealousy, fits of anger, rivalries, dissensions, divisions, (Galatians 5:16–24)*

That is exactly the one bad play in life that I seemed to not be able to overcome. All this time I had been taught about the power of self-control in the sport of football, but could not master this very thing in my personal life. God never interferes with our decision to choose a life of sin over His will to live right in the game of life. We may have had every good intention of doing the right thing, but the truth is we were doing the wrong thing.

My girlfriend and I thought we were doing well, because doing well meant not having drama, gossip, and rumors spread about us. Looking back, I don't know how I could allow myself to be drawn away from all that is right after what my grandfather and mom had taught me all those years.

SPIRITUAL TRUTH: *But every man is tempted, when he is drawn away of his own lust, and enticed. (James 1:4)*

That was the moral compass that I had personally allowed to be set based on my limited experience in the game of life. When we are not living right, we don't get better morally or spiritually, but progressively worse. To be honest, I felt conviction in my heart, but I wanted and liked where I was and the feeling of being with my girlfriend. Because I was doing better in school and football was starting to take off for me, I gave myself the right to make this call in the game of life, a call I knew was not the right play.

Springtime had arrived, and campus life was thriving. It was a time when we should have been experiencing joy, but because of the irresponsible way I was living, negative dividends were starting to pile up in my personal life. Then my girlfriend came to me and said, "Eddie, I am pregnant."

My heart sank. I should have been filled with the joy and celebration of expecting a little one, but we both knew we were not ready. We sat there in silence and she asked me, "What should we do?" Like a coward, I had no answer for her when she deserved one. Emotions flooded my mind and spirit. What am I going to do now? I knew exactly what I wanted to happen. I had run from adversity and problems in the past, but here was my one opportunity to look adversity in the face, deal with it, and be responsible for it.

I looked at her and said, "What do you want to do?" Knowing how much she loved me and I loved her, I could not possibly tell her that I wanted her to terminate the pregnancy. Even the thought of it hurt my heart. I definitely did not want to hurt her, but she deserved an honest answer. We sat there trying to figure out what to do not only with the pregnancy, but also with how her parents would deal with the fact that she had gotten pregnant by an African-American athlete. There was so much to deal with, and it started with our parents. I said, "What do you think your mom and dad will think?"

She responded, "I believe they will support me, but they will be extremely disappointed that I blew my scholarship opportunities." This made the problem that much worse, and by now I was thinking about the bigger effects of how the decision to sleep together was affecting us now that we had this major play to face in the game of life. I said to her, "I just don't think I could live with the possibility of you losing your scholarship, upsetting your parents, and the dream of playing the sport you love. Plus I know that we both are not ready to be parents." I never told her that we should not have the baby. I just could not bear to see her reaction.

But saying what I said took her to another level emotionally. She became angry and said, "I will simply take the pill to ensure it is taken care of." A part of me was relieved, but I was hurt because she was hurt. We both sat there in silence, still unsure, upset and crying.

SPIRITUAL TRUTH: *He that covers his sins shall not prosper: but whoever confesses and forsakes them shall have mercy. (Proverbs 28:13)*

I said, "Sweetie, we can keep it." Although she and I both wanted to, we both knew we were not ready, and we made one of the hardest calls in the game of life we ever had to make. Not only did this call affect our relationship emotionally, but it also had a profound effect on us mentally and spiritually. My mind and heart wrestled that day and many days after with the fact that we made a call that truly was only God's to make. If only we had chosen to live our lives the way God intended, saving sex for the day of our marriage and avoiding all these short term calls in the game of life that produce such horrible consequences. We spend more time wrestling in our flesh because we are living life in our own authority, instead of the power that rests in His.

SPIRITUAL TRUTH: *Flee from sexual immorality. Every other sin a person commits is outside the body, but the sexually immoral person sins against his own body. (1 Corinthians 6:18)*

Had I just applied this spiritual truth to my life, I would never have had to make this hard call. It is really that simple, but so serious at the same time. We have the ability to choose what God wants over our own lustful desires. God has given us all the power to make the right call, but the choice is still ours. Know that even as he empowers us to be the coach in our lives and key moments in the game of life, there are also consequences to every call that we make.

CHAPTER 14

HOW THE LORD'S WISDOM ABOUNDS OVER OUR CIRCUMSTANCES

THE LORD ALLOWED ME to go through so many circumstances over the course of my eighteen years. It appeared that I loved to learn things the hard way. Even though I had seen the devastation and abuse our family had gone through and the big mistake I made in high school, I was now faced with the decision of whether to keep the baby. It was as if I just did not get it. God was obviously using so many circumstances to teach me how to make the right calls in the game of life, but instead of adhering to the wisdom He was trying to teach me, I deliberately chose foolishness.

> **SPIRITUAL TRUTH:** *For the wisdom of this world is foolishness to God. As the Scriptures say, 'He traps the wise in the snare of their own cleverness.' (1 Corinthians 3:19)*

I was relying on the foolishness of my own wisdom, thinking it could teach me how to play the game of life. Yet all I got in return was one heartache and mistake after another, which was truly leading me down a path to losing in life. It was really sad that instead of just taking the time to truly reflect on my life and the decisions I was making, I chose to despise wisdom and embrace the foolishness that was bound in my own heart. What was it going to take?

How many times have we all been there, where we make these bone-headed decisions, and then we turn right around and make more? Shortly after that my girlfriend and I decided to terminate the pregnancy; our reward for that game-time decision was an overflow of guilt and shame. I felt pulled back into a place I thought I had escaped, only to realize that the pain that had laid dormant for so long would resurface and prove to be the strongest opponent I had ever faced.

SPIRITUAL TRUTH: *O God, You know my foolishness; and my sins are not hidden from You... Because for Your sake I have borne reproach; shame has covered my face. (Psalms 69:5,7 NKJ)*

The shame I felt paralyzed me and made me feel the way I felt when I had played a bad game. I wrestled in my mind about my mistakes and carried that same mindset into the next game, never really recovering, not because I was not capable, but because I could not see anything great inside of myself because of this terrible act that I had done. I started to head down a downward spiral, and the only person who knew about it was me—and God. When it comes to the game of life, the worst thing we can ever do is try to battle through what we may be facing on our own. The Lord wanted me to learn from it, not continue to live one bad decision after another. He was looking for me to learn from my mistakes, reflect upon them, and move forward. Truly what was causing the shame was the fact that I could not forgive myself, I felt I had let my girlfriend down, and ultimately I felt like a loser. It all appeared to be natural, but that is not how God sees us, nor desires for us to respond when we are faced with trials that seem insurmountable.

SPIRITUAL TRUTH: *In all this you greatly rejoice, though now for a little while you may have had to suffer grief in all kinds of trials. (1 Peter 1:6)*

I really had nothing to hold onto. When I should have been searching after something spiritually to bring me out of this place of mental defeat, I simply could not. The opponents of shame, guilt, and depression were winning on the front lines, pushing me back and taking me to places from which I felt like I could not return. What was it going to take to pull me out of this place?

It was all coming to a head for me, and I was beginning to realize that after eighteen years of living, I had become the very thing I never desired: I had become just like my father. I had become this narcissistic, hurt, angry, and selfish person who would rather live in pain than accept God's peace. The idea of winning, in my mind, was not walking in integrity but in deceit, hoping that the bad calls I made would not lead to severe consequences in the game of life. I could not take this overwhelming feeling anymore, and I sought the only person I knew who could pull me out of this. God always sends someone who is salt and light for us in key moments in the game of life to help us overcome all that we may be facing. So as I entered the field house, emotionally weary, I walked up the stairs to his office. It felt like an eternity as I walked down the hallway, looking at all of the plaques, creeds, and winning traditions and history of our university and football team. How could I be surrounded by such a winning environment and still be losing in the game of life?

SPIRITUAL TRUTH: *If you try to hang on to your life, you will lose it. But if you give up your life for my sake, you will save it. (Matthew 16:25)*

His door was closed and I was hoping that he would not be there, to be honest, because while I needed help, I was not ready for the truth of what he might tell me.

I knocked on the door lightly, as if not to disturb him. I knocked three more times, but a little harder each time, and behind the door I heard this Southern twang say, "C'mon on in."

I peeped in the door and said, "Coach, is it okay for me to come in?"

He said, "Yes sir, son, come on in. What can I do for you?"

"Coach, I have some issues—"

Before I could get another word in, he said, "Eddie, we are proud of your progress as a player and excited about what you are doing on the field."

I said, "Thank you coach." My spirit brightened up a bit from his comments, but after my words, he immediately knew I was not there to talk to him about football. I said, "Coach, I have made some horrible decisions in my life."

He looked me dead in my eyes and said, "Eddie, we all make mistakes."

Then I said, "Coach, not mistakes like this."

He said, "There is nothing under the sun that God cannot handle or forgive." And at this point I just knew that God could not possibly forgive or accept me in the state that I was in. Coach asked me directly, "What is it that you are facing right now Eddie?"

"Coach, at this point I just can't share what it is. I was so ashamed." What I was really afraid of was disappointing him, as I had so much respect for him. But I could not bring myself to tell him specifically what it exactly was.

He looked at me and said, "Eddie, do you believe God loves you?"

I said, "Coach I don't know."

"Eddie, He loves you more than you could ever imagine. In fact, whatever you are facing cannot be bigger than the love He has for you."

I said, "Coach, God could not love me for what I have done." So he took me to a scripture.

SPIRITUAL TRUTH: *For all have sinned and fall short of the glory of God, being justified freely by His grace through the redemption that is in Christ Jesus, whom God set forth as a propitiation by His blood, through faith, to demonstrate His righteousness, because in His forbearance God had passed over the sins that were previously committed, to demonstrate at the present time His righteousness, that He might be just and the justifier of the one who has faith in Jesus. (Romans 3:23–26)*

He said, "Do you know what this means?"

I said, "No, Coach, I really don't."

"It means that there are no perfect games played out in the game of life. God already knew we could not be perfect, so He sent His son to play it out for us. So when we do mess it up, we don't have to spend the rest of our lives beating ourselves up over the last bad play we have made in life."

My spirit broke and tears started to well up in my eyes, because those words spoke directly to my heart. Those words gave me some sense of hope, that although I had put myself in some very bad situations, there really was not anything that I could have done that could supersede the work of the Cross and blood that Jesus Christ shed for us. Coach looked at me and said, "All it takes is faith to believe, son." It was the first time in my life that I gave myself the chance to believe that the possibility of hope that lived in the redemptive power of the cross could be the greatest play that God had ever given me to run in the game of life. It gave me the ability to believe that there was no circumstance or problem that we face that was ever too big for God.

Coach looked at me and said, "Do you understand now son?"

I said, "Yes, coach. I get it. There really are no perfect plays or games played, except the one that Christ ran on Calvary. Thank you for helping to heal my heart today."

SPIRITUAL TRUTH: *The Lord is near to the broken-hearted and saves the crushed in spirit. (Psalm 34:18 ESV)*

CHAPTER 15

WHO DO YOU REALLY WANT TO BE?

COLLEGE HAD PRESENTED a lot of ups, downs, and game-time decisions where I had to make some serious calls. Overall it had been a great experience. I had built some really solid relationships, had a good plan in place for my future, and gained a lot of wisdom, but my relationship with God was still not that strong. I knew about God, but did not really know God, and as my time in college was coming to an end, it was time for me to make some very real life decisions that would determine the direction in which I would go in the game of life. Although I had a plan, I was not clear as to my purpose.

SPIRITUAL TRUTH: *Many are the plans of a man's heart, but it is the Lord's purpose that shall prevail.*

One of the major reasons I was not clear about my purpose was because I had avoided really getting to know who I was. I was afraid of who I was and the identity of who I might be. Most of that was because I had wrestled with coming to grips and dealing with much of the pain that lived not only in my head, but also constantly resurfaced from my heart when I was put in the right situation. I simply had not come to a place of who I really wanted to be. I knew I wanted to be successful, but at what? I could play football, was on my way to graduating, had a great base of friends, and had a great mom and grandparents, tremendous coaches, and a wonderful girlfriend in Sonya. By all accounts in the game of life, I felt like I was in great condition. But most of my identity was not in growing up in God, but in the sport I played.

> **SPIRITUAL TRUTH:** *I was in them and you are in me. May they experience such perfect unity that the world will know that you sent me and that you love them as much as you love me. (John 17:23)*

I had identified with so many things in my life, whether it was people, the sport I played, tribulation, and even victory. Still, through all this, I had not identified with Jesus Christ. This is what had caused me to wrestle with myself and become my own worst enemy in the game of life. I really did not need any other opponent on the field of life, as I was already an All-Pro at beating myself up. But I still needed to figure things out. My plan was to be a great football player and a great person who helped my family and others.

These were all great goals, and those were only set because they were the things that made me feel good about myself. Being a great football player was what brought me attention from other people, and I had become addicted to that more than being addicted to my relationship with God.

How many of us have been at this place in life where everything we do is to please others? Where the decisions we make are based more on making them happy instead of ourselves, simply because we do not know who we are?

Well, it came down to this moment as we were flying back from Texas after playing in the Sun Bowl. I had just had the game of my life, and although we had lost, I knew this one important fact: My life was about to go through a season of transition, and although I had a plan, I needed to be sure that I was walking in God's purpose.

How many of us have made decisions during times in our life based on these three factors?

- ✦ You made the decision based on an emotional feeling.

- ✦ You made the decision based on your identity in what you do.

- ✦ You made the decision purely out of trying to prove your worth or value to someone else.

That is exactly what I was doing. Although I had a very strategic plan to go to graduate school, I also had so much insecurity about my future. On the flight back, I was so nervous, not about life, but about what my coach might say once I asked him the question about my intent to play professional football. I had been coached by him all these years and had a pretty good idea what his honest opinion was about me. I respected his opinion almost to a fault. I mustered up the courage to walk up to him on the long flight back from Texas, and as I got closer to him, I could see he was visibly upset and agitated over the loss. My timing was probably not right, but the anxious energy I was feeling to know his thoughts would not allow me to rest. I reached his seat and tapped him on the shoulder and said these words: "Coach, can I speak with you for a moment?" He responded, "Of course, son, what do you want to talk about?" I responded, "Coach, I was considering playing professional football and wanted to know what you thought about that."

I was asking him because I looked up to him and he was like a father figure to me and I valued his opinion.

He turned to me and said, "Eddie, I do not think that you could play pro, as I think you are a little undersized, but you do have so many other leadership qualities that no matter what you decide to do in life, you will succeed." Now in defense of my coach, he was not telling me that to break my spirit; he just gave me an honest answer. I was crushed, because the only words I heard him say was "I don't think you can play pro." I turned to my coach and said, "Thank you."

I wanted so much to hear him say, "You can do it, Eddie." I had longed for the voice of a father to tell me, "You can do it, son."

After having the game of my life and being excited about the possibilities of my future, my dream to play pro was crushed. I was dejected and walked back to my seat as though all was lost. I climbed over my teammate and sat back down into my window seat. My teammate asked me, "Is everything okay?"

I didn't say a word. I simply looked out the window at the clouds and gently fell asleep. I did not sleep very long because of the noise of the airplane, but when I awoke, a powerful thought came to me, and it was then that I told myself, "I am going to play pro!" I did not care what coach thought—I was playing pro. In fact, my goal was to prove him wrong, and what he thought would discourage me only encouraged me to make that decision. But I still did not know who I was.

This inspired me to set some definitive goals for my life, but we have to be careful that the pride of life does not sneak in and steal the glory that the Lord deserves from all we do in life. Because although the Lord desires for us to become all things to all men, He does not want us to be so consumed with proving them wrong that we lose sight of the greater purpose that He is trying to establish within the plan we may have for our lives.

> **SPIRITUAL TRUTH:** (In scripture Paul became all things to all men, but he did it for a purpose.) *Though I was free and belong to no one, I have made myself a slave to everyone, to win as many as possible. To the Jews I became like a Jew, to win the Jews. To those under the law I became like one under the law (though I myself am not under the law), so as to win those under the law. To those not having the law I became like one not having the law (though I was not free from God's law but am under Christ's law), so as to win those not having the law. To the weak I became weak, to win the weak. I have become all things to all people so that by all possible means I might save some. I do all this for the sake of the gospel that I may share in its blessings. (1 Corinthians 9:19-23 NIV)*

In that moment that coach told me, "I could not play pro." I was more focused on proving Him wrong than on approaching the circumstance with a mindset of gratefulness and thanking coach for being honest with me.

How many of us have done that—had a dream we wanted to accomplish and instead of becoming who the Lord desires for us to be within the dream He has given us, wind up becoming people who are more reactionary and moved by our anger to prove man wrong instead of proving God and His word to be right? So the question is, will you rise above and make the right call of becoming who God has called you to be in the game of life? Or will you be the person who goes through life focused on proving others wrong and using that as your motivation to accomplish success in life, because who you want to be and who God expects you to be are two totally different things. Following God requires commitment to honoring His purpose within the plan of who He has called for us to be.

I had to realize that although Coach's comments upset me, he was only speaking the truth. Although he could not see God's plan for my life, it was my faith to align my vision with God, to believe that although Coach could not see the greatness in me, God did. If we truly desire to become the man or woman of God that he desires for us to be, we will have to activate our faith to focus more on God's plan for our life and on the fact we can do nothing apart from him. We will have to make the call to ensure that we are not motivated by the wrong reasons, but committed to moving in God's spirit, which keeps us so humble and focused that everything we do in life is to honor the Lord and His word and share in the blessings that come from it.

I came to a place of rest in the vision of God's purpose within the plan, after many months of training. I went back to coach right before the draft to thank him for all he had done for my life, for inspiring me and motivating me to go after my dream. It took tremendous humility to do this. But this is one of the key characteristics that is necessary if we truly want to become who God has called us to be, not only for ourselves, but also for others. We have to walk in a spirit of humility that is not boastful or proud but grateful and thankful for all the Lord has placed in our lives. Make the right call in your life that proves the Greater Goodness that comes from becoming who God has called you to be, instead of being motivated to prove your value to man from the pride that is in your heart.

CHAPTER 16

SUCCESS REALLY DOES NOT FEEL LIKE SUCCESS

HOW MANY OF US have desired to experience success in life, but have a vision of success that has everything to do with getting the job of our dreams, making a lot of money, and then being the person that everyone looks up to? So many of us look at life as a plan, instead of being driven with a purpose, which gives us a false view of who God is really calling us to be.

By this time I was in intense training for the NFL Draft. My mind was so focused and intent on making the NFL that there was nothing distracting me. I wanted to succeed so badly that nothing could have kept me from accomplishing that goal. What kept me driving forward were the words, "You will never play in the NFL." Now, although I was working hard, I really was not working for the right purpose or in the right spirit, for God always desires for all we do to honor Him.

> **SPIRITUAL TRUTH:** *And whatever you do, in word or deed, do everything in the name of the Lord Jesus, giving thanks to God the Father through him. (Colossians 3:17)*

The day finally arrived and it was time to perform. Here we were in front of all thirty teams. We were changing into our workout gear for the day of our lives. As we got dressed, a gentleman from the NFL came in and announced, "Gentlemen, please note that we are excited to be here at your training facility. Remember to give your best. Ask questions if you need to, and most importantly remember the NFL is a once in a lifetime opportunity." What a reality check! My dream was finally coming true. It was not a dream anymore. The best part was that I felt really prepared.

As we started to walk out toward the weight room, our strength coach and emotional leader gave us this speech of encouragement. He said, "Men, you were born for this day, prepared emotionally and physically, and there is nothing that will get in your way. You will be strong and mighty today, as this is the one day that God has prepared you for your entire life. There is no more time to question, doubt, or fear, as all you have is this moment. It is your time to get what you deserve and change your life forever. Don't leave anything on the table. Leave it all out there on the field and in the weight room, men!"

How could I not be ready after that? I knew this was going to be a great day. We formed the line for our weigh-ins and measurements. The gentleman leading the combine called out all our numbers loudly to the host of teams that were there. He yells, "Eddie, Mason, 6'1" 232." Filled with nervous energy but also confidence that was committed to this day, we entered the weight room filled with NFL scouts watching our every move. With each event we had to perform, nothing was better than the event they had all come to watch. Here I was, in this moment that I had really never imagined up until that plane ride back from Texas. Of course I looked up to football players as a young student athlete, but this was actually my chance to experience success at a higher level. There was nowhere to run or hide, no time to think about my painful past, the mistakes, and the unresolved personal issues I had. It was time to seize the moment.

That is exactly what I did as I set myself up to run my first 40-yard dash. I walked up to the line and looked up to see all these NFL scouts looking at me. The feelings were overwhelming in that moment, but exhilarating at the same time. In that split second, although I knew I was ready, there was still that little bit of doubt, which was exactly why I needed to tell myself, "Be great today!" I set myself in my stance as Allen Johnson had taught me to do, looked up one more time, and took off. I knew the moment I left my start point that it was going to be a fast time. As I crossed the finish line and I jogged back with confidence in my heart. I heard one of the scouts say, "What did you get?" Another answered, "4.47. Fast." Another said, "Who is this kid?" Another replied, "I don't know, but we need him to run again!" I had garnered the attention of these men, which I had longed for: to feel respected and wanted and to have someone appreciate the skill set that God had given me. I thought to myself, "All the hard work has paid off."

I had attracted the attention of the San Francisco 49ers, Kansas City Chiefs, and Cleveland Browns for private work-outs. I was surely on my way to doing great things, making a lot of money, and being counted in the ranks of what was defined as success. At least I thought that was the case.

All my workouts, pre-draft tryouts and interviews were done, and I sat on the couch of my girlfriend's apartment. We were hosting a draft party cookout for some of my other team-mates who were potential draft selections as well. A couple of my teammates had already been picked. As the day got longer and the rounds began to pass, I wondered if it was going to happen. The third round went by, then the fourth, then the fifth, and I was thinking, "This is not going to happen." All the work, all the labor, and maybe my coach was right. I got a call from one of my cousins and he said, "Hey cuz, are you getting drafted? It's almost over." I responded, "I hope so, man, all I can do is pray and wait." He said, "I hope you do." I said,

"It's out of my hands." Then my cousin asked the big question: "What are you going to do if you don't get drafted?" I say, "Just go back to grad school." He said, "Ooh," as if to say, "That's it!"

I said goodbye to my cousin. I was really questioning and doubting the entire process by this time. Was I good enough? Did the scouts really like me? I really did not want to be rejected again.

The nervous energy I felt was beyond stressful, and as I said before, I had so many feelings; some were excitement from the potential of being drafted, and others were anxiety that had me worried that my dream was not going to happen.

In all honesty, I needed this to happen for a number of reasons. I wanted to feel what success felt like after working so hard to be drafted. I needed the money, as I had no job opportunities in front of me since my main focus for the last six months had been on this one day. My mind had been so scarred over the years that the fear of rejection paralyzed my level of expectation to believe that what God had placed in front of many could actually happen.

SPIRITUAL TRUTH: *Why are you cast down, O my inner self? And why should you moan over me and be disquieted within me? Hope in God and wait expectantly for Him, for I shall yet praise Him, my Help and my God. (Psalms 42:5)*

Just as I had done so many times before, I started to mentally beat myself up, and Sonya could tell the stress was increasing. The fifth round was coming to a close and there were only two more left. Sonya grabbed my hand and looked me directly in my eyes and said, "It's going to happen, baby." I felt a peace come over me. I really let go at that moment. For the first time, I really turned the opportunity over to God. There was nothing else I could do. I wanted success so much that I forgot that all our blessings come from the Lord, and if this were going to happen, God would have to be the one to do it.

My cousin and roommate Kawana, who was my greatest fan and cheerleader in the game of life since we were kids, said, "Don't worry about all those who doubt you cuz. Because you have worked too hard, and I believe in you." Now the mental drama that would have played out in my mind started to get smaller, and my faith and confidence started to get bigger. Just as we were watching the news ticker on ESPN, they announced the start of the sixth round. Two more rounds to go. The pressure was building. The focus in my mind was not on how this was going to honor God, but what people would think if I did not get drafted. I would be a failure in their eyes. What about helping my family and all the people I loved? My dream of being drafted and experiencing success dimmed with each passing moment my faith started to waiver.

Then finally my agent called and said, "Stay ready; everything is going to work out; you will make it." He reassured me they had been on the phone with several teams and it could happen in any moment.

Sonya asked, "Who was that?"

I said, "My agent just letting me know it is going to happen." Although that made me feel better, I was seriously worried. I wanted to be a blessing to my mom, grandparents, and Sonya, as they had all been such a blessing to me in so many ways. My dream was so close, but so far away.

Then I got the first call and a very calm voice on the other side, said, "Hello, this is the San Francisco 49ers and we are about to draft you with our next pick." I thought to myself, oh my God, it was really going to happen. Then the Tampa Bay Buccaneers called, and they told me they were going with their next pick. My heart started racing. I looked at Sonya and said, "It's going to happen, baby." Kawana started yelling. I had so many thoughts by now, and my heart was racing. I could see the numbers on the ticker tape as they rolled by. Pick number 176 rolled by and the team made the selection. The Minnesota Vikings have pick 177, New Jets have pick 178, San Francisco has pick 179, and Tampa Bay has pick 180. It looked very clear that I was going to the 49ers. Instead of being excited about what was about to happen, the very first thought that came into my mind was,

"I am going to have to move all the way to California." I felt a knot in my stomach, because the reality was I was a young man, and not just a young man, but one who still had a lot of fears, questions, and doubts about who I was. When I should have been thanking and praising God for what was before me, being excited in the moment, I had this feeling of ungratefulness, worry, and fear about the possibility of being relocated all the way to California. The 49ers had just won the Super Bowl, so how could I not be excited? But I wasn't. Success was staring me in the face, and all I felt was sad. When I should have been rejoicing and thanking God for the opportunity and the potential of the success that lived within the chance of being drafted, I was instead worried about where I was going to live.

SPIRITUAL TRUTH: *Rejoice always, pray without ceasing, give thanks in all circumstances; for this is the will of God in Christ Jesus for you. (1 Thessalonians 5:16–18)*

As soon as the thought entered my mind, I got another call. I looked at Sonya and said, "Baby it looks like I am going to the 49ers." I felt excited, but also sad. I am also thinking about our relationship and how it would be affected. I picked up the phone expecting it to be the 49ers, but this time there was a different voice on the phone. The very quiet but confident voice of Mr. Bill Haley (General Manager for the New York

Jets) said, "Eddie, this is Bill Haley. I wanted to ask you, are you ready to be a Jet?"

I said, "Yes, sir! I am so excited for the opportunity to come and play for your team."

He said, "We are drafting you right now," and it was at that moment that my name blinked on the screen, pick number 178.

I said to Mr. Haley, "Thank you for believing in me and choosing me. I will make you proud."

"I know we are very excited to have you as part of our New York Jet family." It was at that moment it hit me that all the training, hard work, sacrifice, and dedication were paying off. But although I was happy on the outside, I was not happy on the inside. Something was missing. Why did I have such a feeling of emptiness?

SPIRITUAL TRUTH: *I say to the LORD, 'You are my Lord; apart from you I have no good thing.' (Psalm 16:2)*

I felt such emptiness at what appeared to be my greatest moment of success in the game of life because I had absolutely no intimate connection to God. Yes, I had everything in front of me that in the eyes of man was as high as you can go in the sport. The likelihood of me even having the opportunity to play in the NFL was slim to none—the chances were literally at .0068%. But there I sat, empty and frustrated with the fact that I even felt that way. The whole time I was thinking, when I get there, my life is going to change. But apart from God, we really cannot do anything in the game of life. We can seek after so much stuff, have so many dreams that are beyond our wildest imagination that we desire to accomplish, but then the dream is achieved, and because God was never an integral part of the process, we feel empty. I did not feel fulfilled because even though I was experiencing success, I had not come to a place in my life where God's purpose was leading my plan.

Take a moment to think about your life for second. Think of a time where you were planning to do something very big and you put so much time and effort into it that at the end of it, you thought it would bring you an amazing feeling of joy and pride. And although for a moment you were excited, you were not moved!

This happens because our lives were not meant to be poster boards of accomplishments, but instead instruments of impact that leave lasting impressions of our relationship with God and understanding of His purpose and plans. Although I had this amazing opportunity in front of me with the New York Jets that could possibly lead to great success, due to my lack of commitment to understanding the greater purpose of why God opened the door beyond just playing football, it simply did not feel like success.

What should have been the happiest moment of my life was just a temporary moment of excitement. This is why in all we do, if our success does not honor God, it will never feel like success until God becomes the ultimate player in the greater purpose of what He has called us to do.

> **SPIRITUAL TRUTH:** *On the contrary, who are you, O man, who answers back to God? The thing molded will not say to the molder, 'Why did you make me like this,' will it? Or does not the potter have a right over the clay, to make from the same lump one vessel for honorable use and another for common use? (Romans 9:20–21)*

We are to be vessels that honor Him, and in doing so all we do will be successful, regardless of how it feels.

CHAPTER 17

VOICES IN THE LOCKER ROOM

OUR LIVES are always going to come down to one thing when it comes to serving God with a whole heart: our ability to make either the right call or the wrong call.

> **SPIRITUAL TRUTH:** *But if you refuse to serve the LORD, then choose today whom you will serve. Would you prefer the Gods your ancestors served beyond the Euphrates? Or will it be the Gods of the Amorites in whose land you now live? But as for me and my family, we will serve the LORD. (Joshua 24:15)*

We run plays every day in the game of life. We must decide to choose the right direction to go, and making the right call has to do with our relationship with God and the examples of others that have been set. As my life was progressing and as

I was experiencing what some would consider success, I was starting to see many good and bad examples of how to live my life. Although I had had some great examples in life, I still had an internal struggle of never feeling like I had that father to teach me about how to be a man in the bigger game of life. At this point I had the experiences of the locker room, then the example of my grandfather's words of wisdom as a guide for choosing which path I was going to take. I had one voice coaching on the possibilities of God's destiny and another wrestling with fulfilling the desires of this newfound lifestyle wrapped in what we call success. So many choices, voices, and examples. Whom do I follow? Everything seemed okay, and besides, no one was doing anything that bad. I mean, I had never had this type of money, been around so many talented people, seen so many nice cars, and walked in so many homes the size of apartment buildings. I was now in a life that I honestly knew nothing about, except for the fact that we all played football and that was why we all had the opportunity to be there. Just like in college, I had learned how to be successful on the field, but off the field my life was a mess. I did not have a clue how to live, because as much of a leader as I had become in the sport of football, I was a follower in the game of life, searching for affirmation and to be loved, respected, and have a voice that everyone looked to. This is where the battle always begins when it comes to our lives.

This day was like any other. We were getting ready for practice, and as I sat there listening to the many voices that were in the room, I heard several conversations: one about what girl someone slept with last night, another of someone talking about the Lord, and another conversation about taking a product to help with performance, and another about a big party and how it was a blast last night. Amidst all the voices of what appeared to be success, I had to choose which one I was going to follow, and on top of that I had to be able to juggle the professional demand that was required to play in the NFL.

SPIRITUAL TRUTH: *There are, it may be, so many kinds of voices in the world, and none of them is without meaning. (1 Corinthians 14:10)*

Listening to all these voices in the locker room, I knew I was going to have to choose which one to listen to. All of them had meaning, whether negative or positive, and what each person was talking about at that point highlighted what was important to them. Although I had the opportunity to establish my own voice in the midst of this locker room, I wanted to fit in. The major issue working against me in the game of life was my insecurity. Had I really taken the time to strengthen some of the spiritual muscles within the Word of God that my grandfaather and mother placed inside of me? It would have made me a lot stronger to handle the pressure of fitting in with the NFL. But that was not the case. I sat there after practice, searching for the right voice that would be common and familiar ground to what I had been accustomed to. Most of the time, we gravitate to things and places that are comfortable. We start searching for that voice or voices that speak to the condition of where our hearts are.

So I heard this voice say, "Hey man, I was going out to Burgundy's tonight to get some drinks, is there anyone who wants to go?" As my teammate looks around speaking to the other veterans, he looks directly at me and said, "Hey rook (meaning rookie), do you want to go?" Now the question he asked me took a split second, but it seemed like an eternity, because he was not just asking me to a bar; spiritually, emotionally, and physically, I was about to draw a line in the sand showing who I wanted to be known as.

> **SPIRITUAL TRUTH:** *...But because of your stubbornness and unrepentant heart you are storing up wrath for yourself in the day of wrath and revelation of the righteous judgment of God, who **will render to each person according to his deeds:** to those who by perseverance in doing good seek for glory and honor and immortality, eternal life;...(Romans 2:5–7)*

Although this seemed like an insignificant moment, it was a defining moment as to what I had placed my value in all these years. It was the accumulation of letting all that time go by when I could have been establishing my identity in Jesus Christ but was busy trying to fit in with the crowd. Now that I had been blessed with this amazing opportunity to play in the NFL, I could have finally chosen the right voice to follow in this new start in life. I sat there in the front of my locker and could have easily said no, but instead I looked right at my teammate and said, "Yes." So all of us finished getting dressed after practice, and instead of going to watch film of practice and trying to improve as a player and then go home, eat and rest, just as I had routinely done since arriving in the NFL, I chose to go to the bar with him.

As we drove to the bar, another voice started to yell within me—the voice of my grandfather, who had always been a man of great integrity and humility. I remember before I had left to go to New York, we had had the opportunity to sit down and talk about life. It was such an intimate conversation between the two of us on the porch of the house we lived in for so many years. It was both humbling and yet profound that God would meet us in this special moment of discussion where my grandfather was trying to coach me up on how to play the game of life and the reasons why I should choose to make the right choices by listening to God's voice over my own. My grandfather, whom I had looked up to all my life, shared these words with me, "Son, please make sure that you keep

God first. Be a man of your word and one of integrity in all you do." I responded, "Grandpa, I will." But he looked at me intently with those light brown eyes, his face bronzed from all those years working and farming in the sun, and the strength within the blood of his Cherokee heritage and said to me, "Life is going to present you with all types of opportunities, son, but the only ones that will matter are the ones that glorify God. If it is not God-honoring and God-fearing, there will be no good value in it, and it will ultimately bring you down. I share this son, because my life has not been perfect. I have made a lot of mistakes in regards to infidelity, as well as drinking for many years. But I made the choice to listen to God's voice and give my life totally to Him without reservation for the exact purpose of bringing honor to His name. I knew my life had no value unless it honored God. I want your life to do that son. Do you hear me?" I responded, "Yes, grandpa, yes sir, I hear you!" He handed me a Bible, and said, "Rely on this as your strength and playbook for life!"

Yet here I was in my car driving down to Burgundy's bar, my grandpa's voice was screaming louder than the voice of invitation to come down to the bar. Yet I still continued to drive toward that bar, because I wanted to fit in. Besides, the guy who invited me was an All-Pro linebacker with great success in the NFL. It couldn't be all that bad. I pulled up to the back of the bar, sitting there in this intimate moment, still having a chance to choose the right voice, and then I walked inside that bar, sat down, and started establishing how I was going to play the game of life in the NFL.

> **SPIRITUAL TRUTH:** *Jesus answered, 'You say correctly that I was a king. For this I have been born, and for this I have come into the world, to testify to the truth. Everyone who is of the truth hears My voice.' (John 18:37)*

But the reality is that my grandfather had given me the truth, and I was buying into a lie—a lie that success was built on a life of partying, drinking, and lack of discipline. One voice was screaming the truth and the other a lie. I was going to listen to one, but ultimately it was going to be my call. I didn't realize that this one defining moment would affect the rest of the game of life that was playing out right before me.

CHAPTER 18

DON'T EVER SAY
WHAT YOU WON'T DO...

HAVE YOU EVER had a moment in your life where you looked at someone else's failures and said, "I will never do that," only to realize that anything done apart from the glory and goodness of God is bound to fail? Not because it is His will for us to fail, but because we have not acknowledged the true value of relationship and power that comes from serving Him with a whole heart.

> **SPIRITUAL TRUTH:** *"And you must love the Lord your God with all your heart, all your soul, and all your strength." (Deuteronomy 6:5)*

This strength does not come from the physical power of work, nor the mental strength that many of us try to find through trial, and not even our human will of perseverance. Rather, it is a strength that comes from acknowledging our weakness.

We are empowered through God's strength and not our own, because we have developed such a love and dependency on Him that everything we do is not in our own power, but His.

But that was not where my life was. Instead, I found myself heading in a direction and down a path of thinking that although I paid God an occasional visit by reading the Bible my grandfather had given me, going to church on holidays, praying before my meals, and doing some occasional community service to make myself feel better, it was enough to give me the right to make all the calls in my life.

I didn't realize that the life I was living was slowly becoming an instrument to serve sin instead of God.

> **SPIRITUAL TRUTH**: *Do not let any part of your body become an instrument of evil to serve sin. Instead, give yourselves completely to God, for you were dead, but now you have new life. So use your whole body as an instrument to do what is right for the glory of God. Sin is no longer your master, for you no longer live under the requirements of the law. Instead, you live under the freedom of God's grace. (Romans 6:13, 14)"*

I was giving myself the right to think that all my good deeds gave me the right to do bad deeds. I continued to repeat this vicious cycle, never realizing that although at the core I was a good person, my relationship with God was bad. I never communicated with Him, never really developed a sound relationship, but every time I was in trouble I would call on His name. As only like a loving father could do, every time God would answer, because of His unfailing and unconditional love for me. I didn't realize that I was not living in the right fellowship and relationship with God, but rather off of His grace. I thought because all hell had not broken loose in my life that I was just fine—that is, until a downward spiral of my life's choices started to play out in the bigger game of life. It is truly ironic how much we can get caught up in ourselves, especially when we are experiencing tremendous success, and lose every bit of focus on the more important areas in life like integrity, being whole, and living a life worthy of honoring God.

SPIRITUAL TRUTH: *"It is harder for a camel to go through an eye of a needle than for a rich man to get into heaven."*

I never understood this until I entered into my second year of playing in the NFL. I inherited this amazing life, and although I knew it had been given to me by the hand of God, I was doing nothing to honor Him. All I was concerned with was how this new, prosperous life could benefit me. This is where things started getting tricky for me, because instead of allowing God to continue to call the plays in my life, I started to make my own calls. Where I had used close friends, my mom, coaches and grandfather to help guide me in the past, I started becoming prideful and saying I could navigate my life by myself. This became a big problem, because I was telling myself that I could handle things on my own, I needed no one, and I had the internal fortitude to solve any problem by myself. I had learned long ago from my grandfather that in order to be strong you must first become weak. Unfortunately I was doing just the opposite, via the choice of free will, thinking that the choices I made would have no consequences.

This is where my life came to a crossroad, one in which my game plan would either bring me tremendous success or heartache and failure. Either way, it would be solely my choice, because I had not realized that no man can bear fruit or make good calls in life unless he commits his life to God.

> **SPIRITUAL TRUTH:** *I was the true vine, and my Father is the gardener. He cuts off every branch in me that bears no fruit, while every branch that does bear fruit he prunes so that it will be even more fruitful. You are already clean because of the word I have spoken to you. Remain in me, as I also remain in you. No branch can bear good fruit by itself; it must remain in the vine. Neither can you bear fruit unless you remain in me. I was the vine; you are the branches. If you remain in me and I in you, you will bear much fruit;*

apart from me you can do nothing. If you do not remain in me, you are like a branch that is thrown away and withers; such branches are picked up, thrown into the fire and burned. If you remain in me and my words remain in you, ask whatever you wish, and it will be done for you. This is to my Father's glory, that you bear much fruit, showing yourselves to be my disciples. (John 15:1-8)

I thought as long as I was a good person, I could make good calls and this entitled me to govern my life choices and affairs. I didn't realize that the path I was choosing was setting me up for long-term failure. This is when it happened. I had slowly and methodically lived my life out with what I refer to as a calculated approach. Those trips to Burgundy's became more and more frequent. After each practice my teammates and I would go and order wings, beers, and shots. It didn't seem like a big deal, but there was one major thing that was not good. The routine of doing it every day was secretly leading to a problem in my spiritual and personal life. My habit of drinking with my teammates was causing me to look at other women, smoke pot, and I was starting to look for other ways of how to feel the buzz of being high.

All my life I had made these promises to myself: I would never abuse women, never be like my dad and become an alcoholic, never use drugs, never make stupid, irrational choices. Although I had learned how to manage my life, I had not learned how to live and walk the game of life out God's way. I had simply learned how to fight, claw, and scratch my way through life, without any consideration of the consequences ahead, placing a greater value on the appeal of man's approval, diminishing all that I had been taught about how to be a leader and trust God regardless of what my life looked like. My prideful actions were starting to win in my life. I didn't stop for a moment to take an account of the accumulation of the bad plays that were playing out, didn't take a moment to reflect on my life to see what needed to change. I enjoyed living in the moment and owning my own power. I totally dismissed God's wisdom, and the Lord gave me over to myself.

This night as we sat at the bar, the drinks just were not enough. We ordered shot after shot, trying to find that one drink that would take us over the edge, playing drinking games, just like on the field, competing to see who demonstrated the most mental and physical toughness. As I sat there on the bar stool the way I had done so many times before, building up a tolerance for alcohol, I said boisterously, "Man, I am not even feeling this anymore," and slammed the shot glass down on the table. My teammate leaned over to me and whispered, "I got something in my car that will take you higher." I said sarcastically, "What do you have," as if to say there is nothing in your car that could ever deal with me. My ego was so big and my pride was terrible. He said, "We'll see." So we got up and started to walk outside. By this time, I was really curious about what he had in his car. Normally I would have questioned myself or my judgment, but the alcohol had given me that liquid courage to not even worry or think about what might be in his car or to rationally think if this was the right thing to do.

We get out to his tricked-out Mercedes and he said, "Get in on the other side and I'm going to take you higher, brother."

I kind of ran to the other side of his car and said, "Man, you better have something good in here." I figured he had some killer pot that we were going to smoke. But what I thought would be a simple few puffs on a joint turned out to be something way more than I could ever expect.

As I got in his car, I could smell weed, so by now I was totally thinking we were going to smoke some pot. Instead, he reached down inside the center console of his car and pulled out a very small piece of aluminum foil. I knew at this point something serious was going down. He opened the aluminum foil and, to my amazement, in broad daylight, behind the tinted windows of his Mercedes, pulled out what appeared to be some white powder. In my mind, just like when I was a kid and I had gotten in that car in high school. Here I was again. I was thinking, *Oh, crap. How in the world did I get here?* He said, "Take a hit, man."

I immediately responded, "Man, I don't do coke."

He was like "That's cool." I watched him cut up two lines and could not believe what I was watching. After he finished we walked back inside the bar and I really began to throw the alcohol and shots back, but never said a word about what had just happened. Although I knew what he was doing was wrong, this guy was making millions, doing coke. So I started to play this mental game out in my head; if he is doing this, going to Pro Bowls and making millions, then maybe this is what I need to be doing. He doesn't appear to be hurting at all. As that mental game played out in my head, never did I realize that it was building momentum in my heart to manifest itself.

SPIRITUAL TRUTH: *For as he thinks in his heart, so is he. (Proverbs 23:7)*

At the bar I began to wrestle back and forth in my head about trying one line of coke. As if on cue, he said, "You ready to go to the city and party?"

I said, "Say what? Man, we have had a lot to drink."

He said, "I am on full alert now, buddy. That's how it makes you feel, like Superman!"

"You serious?"

He said, "Hell yeah I'm serious."

Against even my best judgment, I got right into that car. We were driving to a club in the city, and by this time my alcohol buzz was coming down and he was telling me how coke stays with you and you don't have to drink as much. I was buying all he was saying hook, line, and sinker. As we pulled up to the club, the big question came and he asked, "Do you want to do a hit?"

I look at him and answered, "Why not?" It was the worst call I had ever made in my life. All I had to do was say no, but instead I said, "Yes, but only one line." He prepared the line, and then I snorted it, and as quickly as it went down, so did these emotions and feelings of disgust in my mind and heart. Just like he said it would, I felt like Superman, although with no cape or S on my chest. I had taken myself to a place of no return. Where before I had had some boundaries of things I said I would never do, this took all the barriers and borders down. I really did not care now! My failed relationship and inconsistent love of God finally caught up with me. I had no commitment toward the relationship and didn't realize at the time that this would now be my biggest problem and that it would open up doors of opportunity to do things that I had told myself I would never do.

The playbook my grandfather had taught me to follow in the game of life was being scrapped for one of compromises, poor choices, and irresponsibility. How do people get to these places? Because at the end of the day we all have done things we really regret or wish we would have never done, but what is the root or cause of us letting our guard and discernment down to the point of no return? You may be shocked by the answer, but it is simple. We do it because of selfishness and our inability to surrender our lives to God. Until we come to a place of total surrender to Jesus Christ, we all have the potential to make decisions and do things that we may think in our hearts we are not capable of. Until the reality and truth arises that when we choose to make calls in the game of life based on a temporal outcome, we will always experience long-term pain. Without the power of Christ and His word as our playbook, it is simply going to be too difficult to move forward and make any positive progress in the game of life.

> **SPIRITUAL TRUTH**: *Then he said to the crowd, 'If any of you wants to be my follower, you must turn from your selfish ways, take up your cross daily, and follow me. If you try to hang on to your life, you will lose it. But if you give up your life for my sake, you will save it.' (Luke 9:23, 24)*

CHAPTER 19

HOW DO I TELL HER

ONE OF THE HARDEST THINGS to do is admit when you have messed up. I don't mean messed up a little bit; I mean really blew it to the point that it not only affects your life, but the lives of those you love. I found myself headed back from New York, anxious about my future, trying to forget my past and the very present circumstance I had created after finding out about a pregnancy. In all honesty, after finding out the rumors of my possible pending release from the team, all I was concerned with was getting back to North Carolina. But this gut-wrenching feeling that was in the pit of my stomach over what I had to tell Sonya had me thinking so many thoughts. I was not sure what to do, to be quite honest. My normal mode of playing out difficult situations in my life was just to ignore them. But there was no avoiding this—it was not something I could simply make go away.

SPIRITUAL TRUTH: *When I kept silent, my bones grew old through my groaning all the day long. For day and night Your hand was heavy upon me. (Psalms 32:3–4).*

In my heart I wanted to keep this secret to myself and figure out a way to make the consequences of hurt that I would soon cause to the heart of my fiance and family go away. That is the one thing I had never wanted someone else to go through in the game of life as I did: emotional, mental, and spiritual pain. But it was my time to head home, so I had packed and started the drive back from New York to North Carolina.

As I drove back with so many thoughts in my head, I started to realize that some of the hardest calls we have to make in life are the ones that expose the true nature of who and where we are in the game of life. It is that time of looking in the mirror and realizing that we all are a mess apart from God. It was time to tell her about the baby I was expecting. But how? What was the right way? How will she respond? Will she leave me, cast me down and reject me as my father had done many years ago?

The thought and weight of that is what I contemplated, as that was my greatest fear, the fear of being rejected. This, in all honesty, is the major opponent I had faced in the game of life. But it was time for me to stand up and do what was right, re-gardless of how it was going to make me look, as what was most important was speaking truth out of respect and love for Sonya.

But I did what so many of us do: Live a lie, and not confront the very thing that we need to face.

This was the decision I made selfishly. I was too afraid to deal with telling her as I drove back. I needed to address some unresolved issues with Sonya beyond the pregnancy, as I really wanted our relationship to go to the next level. I loved her very much and did not want to lose her.

When I walked inside our apartment in Durham, I could tell she had grown so much on a personal and spiritual level. She was at such a place of peace, and here I was bringing all this chaos back with me. I tentatively walked into the apartment, with the weight of what I had to tell her, because I had tried to put distance between us to make myself feel better about the sinful life I was living in New York. Here I was, back, ready for a fresh start, hoping to really work on our relationship. I yelled to Sonya, "I'm back!" and acted as if everything was fine.

She responded, "I'm so glad! I missed you." Now imagine, here is this woman I love and I have this secret that I cannot confess because of fear and guilt, yet I carry it, creating a secret divide in our relationship. So I started out by letting her know about the trip I was planning for us to New York for New Years Eve along with two of our closest friends, Mike and Alisia. She jumped up and hugged me, because she only wanted to be a part of my life. Up until this point, I had not included her in the process. She asked, "When do we leave?"

I excitedly told her, "A few days before New Years." She was clearly happy. It seemed as if to her it appeared I was a different person, but in reality I was a fake. I mean, talk about being at an all-time low; I did not think I could get any lower, and my way of escape was the drugs and alcohol I had turned to to numb the pain of carrying this weight.

> **SPIRITUAL TRUTH**: *He who covers his sins will not prosper, but whoever confesses and forsakes them will have mercy. (Proverbs 28:13)*

I had no idea that I was opening myself up to the worst game I would ever play in life by making this bad call. So I chose even outside my own best judgment to keep this secret as we arrived in New York for New Years. There we were in New York, enjoying the city with full VIP treatment, going to all the popular sites, clubs, and restaurants, and deep down in my heart was this secret that only I knew. Although I learned to numb the pain through my addiction, it was only a temporary fix. My game-time opponent was bigger than any drug or drink. The spiritual weight was too heavy for me to carry.

> **SPIRITUAL TRUTH**: *Let us lay aside every weight, and the sin which does so easily beset us, and let us run with patience the race that is set before us. (Hebrews 12:1)*

So as I contemplated the how, when, and where, after having a few drinks I look at my sister who had come with us on the trip, and asked, "How do I tell Sonya that I got another woman pregnant?" She said, "Eddie, you just tell her, don't sugar coat it, just give her the honest truth." I responded, "Thank you big sis, for always being that light." But honesty and integrity were so far removed from my life that I had forgotten how to perform those types of acts. I was simply out of practice of living life the way God had called me to. But I made a decision that I would make the right call when we returned from our trip to New York.

The time had come. We were settled in from our trip and I was sitting on the couch and sweating, nervous, and racing with anxiety. I asked Sonya to come sit beside me. Now I had already sort of ruined the trip to New York by confiding in her about being involved with someone else. I knew as soon as we returned there was going to be a lot of questions in her mind that I would have to answer. Although all I wanted to do was move forward and grow deeper in our relationship, I had a bigger bomb that I was about to drop. The emotions I felt were unbearable, because all I could think about was the day we met. How happy I was, how simple life had become, and how assured I was of our relationship the first time I met her. I reflected on the memory of our first unofficial date at her house watching the NCAA basketball tournament and how she was so nice to me. I thought of all the great times we had spent together and how I knew from the first moment I met her that she was the one. So, with tears in my own eyes, I looked straight into Sonya's eyes, and she said, "What's wrong?"

I took a deep breath and told her about the pregnancy. The sadness that filled that room and the weight and burden that I had carried had now been placed upon her heart. It was a selfish act on my part, and although she deserved the truth, the situation simply was not right. All of this could have been avoided if I had just been living my life out the way God had intended. Making one dumb decision after another and never learning had led me to this moment of hurt.

She asked, "Why, Eddie? Why didn't you tell me when you got back? Why wait and then set me up for all these emotions and give me a chance to choose if I wanted to stay?"

I said, "I don't know, I didn't want to hurt you and I wanted to spend time with you."

She said, "Well, you did a great job with the hurt part. I am so angry, as I wanted to be the one to give you your first child. I need some time."

I really wanted to talk right at that moment, but I would have to be patient.

SPIRITUAL TRUTH: *But they that wait upon the Lord shall renew their strength; they shall mount up*

with wings as eagles; they shall run, and not be wea-
ry; and they shall walk, and not faint. (Isaiah 40:31)

So a few days later, after collecting her thoughts we sat down and began to talk. With so much emotion, tears were streaming from both our faces and I was devastated that I was inflicting on the one person I had true love for the same kind of hurt that had been inflicted on me as a child. I wanted so much to take it back and make it disappear. So I said, "Sonya I am unworthy of your love. You deserve someone who will love and respect you for who you are. Not a selfish person like me. I would rather see you be happy with someone than to be with me, dealing with this." I knew if there were any hope, it would be a long journey.

So she asked, "How long have you been seeing her?"

I responded, "For the season."

She wanted to know every detail to help her understand the mess I had created for her. After hearing all the details, instead of running as I had done so many times before, she turned to me without blinking and said with blind faith, as if she knew something I didn't, "I've made the decision that I am going to stand with you through this, as I love you!" It blew my mind! What love? How? Where does this come from? I had never experienced anything like this before. So many had left me, but she stayed.

SPIRITUAL TRUTH: *In view of all this, make every effort to respond to God's promises. Supplement your faith with a generous provision of moral excellence, and moral excellence with knowledge, and knowledge with self-control, and self-control with patient endurance, and patient endurance with godliness, and godliness with brotherly affection, and brotherly affection with love for everyone. The more you grow like this, the more productive and useful you will be in your knowledge of our Lord Jesus Christ. But those who fail to develop in this way are shortsighted or blind, forgetting that they have been cleansed from their old sins. (2 Peter 1:5–9)*

I realized that day that God's ultimate call in the game of life is for us to allow for love to be perfected even when we are suffering through pain. That although we had a long journey ahead of us, we both were committed to a promise that love would be the one thing that would help us conquer any opposition or opponent that we might have to face as we moved forward in the bigger game of life. A bond was created that day between Sonya and I that would never be able to be broken.

CHAPTER 20

SALVATION

IN LIFE SOMETIMES we all are going to make some very bad calls. Calls that we may regret, want to erase, and wish did not happen. But even in the midst of us choosing to make some really bone-headed decisions, God still is in control. Although we place ourselves in harm's way, the love that Jesus Christ has for us abounds even beyond the boundaries of our poor choices.

> **SPIRITUAL TRUTH:** *"For all things work together for the good of those that love Him and are called according to His purpose." (Romans 8:28)*

God will take all the bad calls we have made in the midst of us deserving judgment for our lack of self control and foolish decision making and still give us the grace to play the game of life out His way.

Even on my worst day, that one decision to use drugs pressed me into a life that I had never wanted to live. Although there were a lot of bad things happening in my life, God continued to provide people who demonstrated the love of Christ, showed me unconditional love, and provided a true picture of what it looked like to live life the way He intended. The Lord was not allowing any excuses and was setting up what would be the biggest call I would ever make in the game of life.

I was preparing to leave New York again after some off-season rehab, not really knowing what was next and injured. I also found out I was an expectant father and I had no contract in sight. The Jets had just announced that they'd hired a new head coach, Bill Parcells, and I wondered what he was going to be like. The legendary Bill Parcells, who had won Super Bowls for the Giants, was now going to be my head coach. But I continued to pack up my stuff, hoping to get back to North Carolina to a place of peace and familiarity. New York had become a playground that had unleashed a whole new team of opponents that were not just trying to advance but to take me out in the game of life. So I wanted out. I wanted to run as far as I could, at least for a little while, until I could wrap my head around all that was taking place. I was wrestling in my head with my present circumstances, as well as with my future. Then my phone rang. On the other end of the line was a very strong Northern accent, and although I had never met Coach Parcells, his voice was very distinctive.

He said, "Eddie, this is Coach Parcells, I wanted you to know son, that we will not be renewing your contract."

I was devastated at this news. Although I wanted to leave New York, I did not want to leave under those conditions. In some ways I felt like I had never had the success that I knew I could have had, if I had not gotten hurt. But I mustered up the strength to tell Coach Parcells, "Thank you so much for the opportunity. I wish you and the organization the best."

Even though I thought I could handle the words of coach Parcells releasing me, it devastated me, and the game of life began to spiral out of control. As soon as I hung up the phone, anger, frustration, dejection, and disappointment set in, and much of the pain I had covered up and buried for so long started to resurface. I knew very well who my opposition was in the game of life: myself. But I was not doing a thing about it. The lifestyle I was leading and the pattern of behavior I was following resulted in my living a life that was becoming one big lie, with no consistency, faith, or anchor to hold on to, because I was getting further and further away from God. All those visits to the bar had unleashed the worst opponent I would have to face in the game of life: my selfish addiction to drugs and alcohol. The drugs and alcohol magnified and made everything appear to be ten times worse than it really was. I wanted to find some level of hope, but the emotional fog did not allow for me to see hope. I started to throw all my stuff into my bags. I was leaving New York for good. On my way out, I stopped by the facility, got my things and saw some people, paid my respects and hit the road, headed back home.

As I was driving back I immediately started to feel the pressure of the circumstances and then sank into depression. An intense game was playing in the battlefield of my mind, and I was questioning everything about myself and reflecting on what had happened and what was next.

> **SPIRITUAL TRUTH**: *Therefore do not worry about tomorrow, for tomorrow will worry about itself. Each day has enough trouble of its own. (Matthew 6:34)*

I reflected back on what seemed like yesterday when Sonya and I were celebrating on the couch of her apartment after I got drafted. For that brief moment a smile came on my face with that memory, but in reality all hell was breaking loose in my life. I felt like there was no way out physically, mentally, and emotionally. I felt trapped, empty, and void of understanding and although I had money in the bank and appeared to have everything, I had nothing.

> **SPIRITUAL TRUTH**: *But those who want to get rich fall into temptation and a snare and many foolish and harmful desires which plunge men into ruin and destruction. For the love of money is a root of all sorts*

of evil, and some by longing for it have wandered
away from the faith and pierced themselves with
many griefs. (1 Timothy 6:9–10)

My focus was on trying to improve my financial status, not my life. I was determined to continue to play the game of football at a high level and the game of life at a fast pace. To be honest, I really was not in any sort of mental condition to take on one more thing. I had enough stress for ten people and probably should have been checking myself into a rehab center. Then my phone rang. On the other end of the line was my great friend and loyal agent, Brian Levy. He said, "Eddie, guess what?"

I said, "What, my friend?"

He said, "I just got off the phone with Tampa Bay and they want to sign you tomorrow. Do you want to go?"

"Hell yeah, I want to go. Florida: sun, football, fishing, and fun. What more could you ask for?" How selfish I was. Here God was opening another door of opportunity, but no thanks or praise went up to God. Instead I asked, "Where do I sign up?"

He said, "You have to get back to North Carolina as soon as possible to get ready to go to Florida to do this deal."

Deep down I knew I did not need to go to Florida, as my life was a mess. I asked him, "What about my ACL?"

He said, "They totally understand about your knee and are willing to wait for you to have a full recovery as they really love your upside."

A big smile crossed my face, but here I was, a drug addict and alcoholic, living a lie, and my agent is working his butt off trying to sell me as a high-character guy to, of all men, Coach Tony Dungy. I took a deep breath, released a sigh of relief, and told Brian, "Let's get it done." I was entrenched in my bad habits and my routine of putting Band-Aids over problems instead of solving them, still in bondage to myself and my old way of thinking,

I went to Tampa, and my fiancé was with me, since she was the one consistent force in my life. That secret life I was living was exactly that: a secret. I actually told myself that no one would ever find out about my drug and alcohol habits. But God loves us so much that He will do whatever it takes to defend and fight for our souls, even if it means us falling from grace in the eyes of man.

> **SPIRITUAL TRUTH:** *For nothing is hidden that will not become evident, nor anything secret that will not be known and come to light. (Luke 8:17)*

My time with the team was going well, and on the surface it seemed as though it was the right fit. My play on the field was improving daily as I trained hard in the weight room, training room, and field to get back to 110% where I was prior to my injury. My focus was so intent on getting back to playing football that I ignored the fact that I was suffering in the game of life. I had done nothing to correct the internal and spiritual injuries of insecurity, pride, arrogance, pain, and depression that I had experienced over the years of going through one trial after another and making foolish choices with my head instead of following the wisdom of God that was in my heart. Those choices, which continued to be the main reason I was losing in the game of life, would prove to be the major cause of why I was not making any personal progress in life. Right when I was thinking I had a handle on where things were, I got blindsided.

I was at home with Sonya, sitting on the couch, when I get a call from a complete stranger. This was not just any call; a deep, raspy, but very serious voice was on the other end. He said, "Am I speaking with Mr. Eddie Mason?"

"Yes indeed, sir. But who is this?"

He responded, "This is Dr. Lombardo, and I am calling about a recent urine sample we received." Although I did not want to imagine what was about to happen, I did know in my gut I was finally going to be found out. He said, "Eddie, your urine sample has come back positive for drugs in your system."

Still in denial and trying to avoid facing the truth, as I had learned so many years to do, I said, "Doc, I don't use drugs, sir, you must have me mixed up with someone else." As Sonya sat there listening to this conversation, it was very evident how disappointed she was, and I knew this was just another moment where I had blown it again. I could have made the right call so many times, but I was still making the wrong ones.

I continued to speak to Dr. Lombardo and question the integrity of this call, as well as the league's system to test these multi-million dollar athletes effectively. He said, "Eddie, we don't make mistakes, so you will have to enter into our substance abuse program to stay eligible to play in the NFL." I hung up thinking, *what am I gonna do now?*

> **SPIRITUAL TRUTH:** *Why, my soul, are you downcast? Why so disturbed within me? Put your hope in God, for I will yet praise him, my Savior and my God. (Psalm 42:5)*

I had built up the façade of a false sense of confidence for so many years, placing all my trust and identity in the sport I played. I had really screwed things up this time. There was no avoiding the consequences of my actions. The more I thought about the fact of what just happened, the more I realized I had to face the truth. Positive drug test, baby on the way, recovering from ACL injury, and then I get another call about thirty minutes after my call with Dr. Lombardo.

This time it was Tony Dungy. He said, "Eddie, this is

Coach Tony Dungy and I need you to come to the facility so we can speak."

I respond, "Yes sir. I will be there in an hour."

He said, "Eddie, I need you here within the next twenty to thirty minutes."

I hopped in my car, sped down to One Buc place, and entered the building, trying to be upbeat and play down the significance of this game-time moment in my life. I knew something really big was about to happen. Here I was at another door of a coach's office, knocking on that door because of some foolish act I had done.

Coach said, "Eddie, how are you doing?"

To me this was a loaded question, because I could have answered it in so many different ways. But my answer was, "Coach, I'm doing pretty good."

He responded, "Do you know why I have you here in my office today?"

This gave me another opportunity to own my mistake. But I took the cowardly way out and responded, "Coach, I'm not sure of the reason."

I could feel a shift in his demeanor at this point that although he was giving me an opportunity to tell the truth, I simply was not ready to face it. So he helped me and stated the facts. "Eddie, we are aware of the positive test that has come back and for that reason as well as others, we are gonna have to let you go." I was devastated. But Coach wasn't finished. He looked me dead in the eye and said, "Eddie, you are such a better man than this and God has so much more for you. Get your life together son, get the help you need and become the football player you were born to be." Finally, someone in my life told me what I needed to hear and did not spare the truth. I broke mentally, spiritually, and physically. Coach Dungy's words were exactly what I needed to hear to awaken my senses and to open up to God's word and spirit. I sat in his office with tears in my eyes, finally coming to the realization of how many years I had played life the wrong way.

I had learned so many life lessons from my mother and grandfather but had applied so few of them. Although I hated getting released from the Buccaneers, it was the best thing that could have happened to me. The Lord knew I was not ready to handle the responsibilities that came with life in the NFL, nor did I have the character necessary to be an ambassador for the blessing that God had placed in front of me. Instead of continuing to fight pridefully for something I was in no condition to handle, I decided to give in. What had seemed so valuable to me was now being taken away. It was not easy to sit back and watch all I had worked for slowly be taken from me, but for every physical thing I lost in the game of life, God was restoring something far greater spiritually.

The major door that had been opened was the invitation to attend Revealing Truth Ministries. My fiancée Sonya started to attend, and I started to despise this newfound religion she had taken on as part of her daily life. We had partied so much together, and now she was becoming a holy roller. I asked her so many times, why, why this church, why now? Each time she replied with loving grace, "To become the woman God called me to be. And you should come with me to church." I told her I was not going to that church. But then I thought about it and wondered if this was the perfect opportunity to go and see why she was so into this church. And even with my negative attitude, as we entered the church, I felt a presence of God that I had never felt before. I tried to find some fault in that church, but I could not find anything. It was a very dynamic ministry that had a heart for people. I noticed such a spirit of excellence in everything this ministry did. I just wanted my old Sonya back.

SPIRITUAL TRUTH: *See, I was doing a new thing! Now it springs up; do you not perceive it? I was making a way in the wilderness and streams in the wasteland. (Isaiah 43:19)*

As I was looking to stay in this old pattern, mindset, and way of life, God was strategically designing the new playbook for how Sonya and I were going to play the game of life. The difficulty was that I had a problem with the perception of this new reality and the truth that God was using Sonya to be that conduit to open my heart to the salvation of God's Kingdom. It really did not matter what I said to her; she had her mind made up that she was moving forward spiritually, with or without me. She was not giving up on me, but she knew if there was any hope for us, we were going to have to get real and get healthy God's way.

So as I was sitting there at church, looking around in amazement at the worship of the people, I could feel an excitement in the air. I was still hoping to find something negative to complain about, but I could not find anything. They treated me as a normal human being and to be honest, that's exactly what I needed. But God had a new game plan for me this day, and it was in the liberty and freedom that came through the salvation through Jesus Christ.

Pastor Powe said, "Many of you are tired, and you have been pulling yourself through life with all these weights, feeling like there is no way out of your situation and circumstance. You are completely tired and exhausted and your heart is at the point of giving up and giving in. You have no more strength and you wonder how you can take another step. Yet God is saying if you take one today, He will give you a new life that is beyond your wildest dreams. He will redeem you back through the blood of Jesus and give you hope to move forward." He continued by saying, "God said if you will act and move in faith and take one step forward, He will begin to restore all that the enemy has tried to steal from you."

He made the altar call, and I was too afraid to go up because I was worried about what people would think. He stated, "If you did not move, still make this confession in your faith with this scripture, right where you are."

SPIRITUAL TRUTH: *That if thou shalt confess with thy mouth the Lord Jesus, and shalt believe in thine heart that God hath raised him from the dead, thou shalt be saved. For with the heart man believeth unto righteousness; and with the mouth confession is made unto salvation. For the scripture saith, Whosoever believeth on him shall not be ashamed. (Romans 10:9–11 KJV)*

I made that confession under my breath, and just as I did, I immediately felt a weight lift off me. This was the beginning of a special moment. After service I felt this stirring in my heart and passion rising up in me that I had never felt before. Back in our apartment, Sonya went back to the bedroom and I remained in the living room. I asked her, "Sonya can you please bring your Bible?" She brought it to me and I found that scripture Romans 10:9–10 as I felt something in my heart of unfinished business. I simply could not stop until

God finished what he had started earlier that day in church. I opened the Bible to the scripture and began to read it and said to God, "If you are real, I want you to touch my hand." I was not asking God as though I did not believe in Him, I was asking for the purpose that I had never had an intimate encounter with God, and this time He exceeded my expectations. As I stated this prayer to God, I felt and saw this hand of light come down and touch my hand. This was all happening in my living room and I was convinced that God did not want there to be any doubt in my heart that He was real and would not be denied and had a special place in His heart for my life.

I broke down and started weeping like never before. I never cried in the past, but this day would be different, as every weight I had was being lifted. A miracle was taking place and God was restoring me, but even more importantly He was saving my soul from the darkness that had surrounded me. A new day was beginning in my life and I was excited to live again, even though there was still so much to figure out. I did not care about all that. All I cared about was the fact that God loved me enough to see me in my little apartment living room and was speaking destiny into me again through the salvation and redemption of the blood of Jesus. It was like being in a game where the score of the opposition was so high that there is no way you could come back, except the one who created the game in the first place gave me the grace necessary to even the score and the playing field. What a blessing to know finally that I was not playing by myself. It was a time of redemption, joy, and salvation, and I would never be the same.

If you are not saved, my prayer is that you would take the time right now to make that confession of your faith to the Lord Jesus Christ and allow for Him to restore all that the enemy is trying to take from you today.

CHAPTER 21

MY EXODUS

SPIRITUAL TRUTH: *"Therefore, say to the people of Israel: 'I was the Lord. I will free you from your oppression and will rescue you from your slavery in Egypt. I will redeem you with a powerful arm and great acts of judgment. I will claim you as my own people, and I will be your God. Then you will know that I was the Lord your God who has freed you from your oppression in Egypt. I will bring you into the land I swore to give to Abraham, Isaac, and Jacob. I will give it to you as your very own possession. I was the Lord!'"* (Exodus 6:6–8)

He had heard my cry from the moment I was in my living room that evening when he saved and redeemed me from the pain of my past. But this did not mean that the journey ahead would come without a cost. God was more concerned about what I learned from the past, so that I did not continue to repeat those patterns of behavior in my future. The process began in my willingness to recognize that I truly had problems and then having a heart and motivation to realize that the only way I was going to move forward was to be able to take on a new mindset that would give me the strength to walk out my future. The physical, emotional, mental, and spiritual bondage I had carried for so long could not go where God was trying to take me.

It was really time for me to transition into a new way of thinking, to make myself available to whatever "half-time adjustments" God was trying to make in my life. Part of that process required that I change the people, places, and things that I had become so accustomed to.

By this time—after being cut, giving my life to Jesus Christ, being faithful in my commitment to church, experiencing true love in marriage, and my drug and alcohol rehab—God also began to strip me of everything that resembled my past, including the thoughts, habits, addictions, pride, and negative attitude that I had made a part of the game of life.

I went to the bank, and it appeared that the money I had made with the New York Jets was getting lower and lower. To be honest, although I had given my life to Jesus Christ, it did not mean that I immediately lost all fear and doubt, especially considering that the majority of my life I had given myself to being confident about what I had and could do, separate from living a life of trust that resided in God. So when I saw that our finances were getting low, fear started to set in. I did not want to be a failure to my wife or make it seem like we could not do the things we used to. I thought that once you got saved and gave your heart to God, my life would simply turn around. But my view of what life looked like and God's view were two totally different things. For the majority of us, when we come into the Kingdom of God and receive God's love and forgiveness through salvation and the redemptive power of the cross, we many times think that is it. But really, that is only the beginning, and that's exactly what I was learning. What I thought I needed, the Lord was revealing more and more that I didn't.

This is when it all started to happen: the first snare in the game of life that God dealt with was my love of status, money, and things. The empowerment I felt when I purchased jewelry, clothes, watches, and drugs made me feel good about myself. It made me feel as though my life had more value, and the more money I could count in my accounts, the better. The number of zeros at the end of each debit receipt made me feel worthy on the outside, but unworthy on the inside. It did not matter how much I had, because it was never enough.

SPIRITUAL TRUTH: *Whoever loves money never has enough; whoever loves wealth is never satisfied with their income. This too is meaningless. (Ecclesiastes 5:10)*

While I thought success was in what you have, God was demonstrating that success to him, when it comes to winning in the game of life, is about who you are.

So as the money got lower and lower, I was putting on this face to Sonya as if everything was all right. We decided to stay in Tampa, as it was a great city. We had an amazing church family and our relationship was the best we had ever experienced.

The reality of knowing we were about to experience financial problems began to set in, and the stress of not knowing our future started to create stress for me. I wondered how to tell Sonya and how was I going to make a living, because I was not ready to give up on my dream of playing. I wondered, now what?

When I should have been seeking God for answers, I took on the old mindset of doing things the only way I knew how. This was to go into survival mode, and instead of trusting that God would provide, I began to rely on myself. I picked up the phone and called one of my old teammates, dreading to even ask, as my mom had taught us to not ask for help but to totally be dependent on God and to figure it out. But I wanted a quick fix, a solution so I could continue to place my trust in the life we had been accustomed to, never realizing that God's whole plan was to strip me of all of that.

I was sitting in my truck outside of the apartment because I did not want my wife to hear my conversation with my good friend and old teammate. As I was dialing the phone, something was tugging at me, and my heart was shouting, "Put the phone down!" But my pride simply would not allow me to.

My friend picked up and said, "Hello, who is this?"

"It's Eddie, man, how are you doing?"

He said, "Great, my brother, and you?"

I said, "Doing great, but going through some things and just trying to figure life out."

Now at this point it was very clear that I was not calling for just a simple hello. In my mind, I was hoping he would help me out, but there was another part of me that really did not want to ask, fearful of the response, because for me, asking for help represented weakness.

My teammate said to me, "How much do you need, brother?"

I said, "I was afraid to ask man. It's not a small amount."

He said, "How much, man?"

"I need five thousand, man!"

After a bit of hesitation, he responded, "Done. I'll send it to you!"

As soon as he said that, I felt pressure leave me. Although that five thousand dollars would help, it would not be the solution, as there were bigger problems that God was trying to sort out in my life.

So I sat there in my truck smiling and feeling better because

I knew this five thousand dollars would help carry us for a while and give me time to continue to train. I got out of my truck and walked into the apartment and the first thing I did was to ask Sonya if she wanted to go celebrate. She asked, "Celebrate what?" I said, "Just life." Just as I had done so many times before, I was keeping secrets because I was insecure about facing the truth of who and where I really was in the game of life. My problem was my fear of showing weakness and looking like I was unable to do something. I wanted to be the hero of sorts in my own eyes, when God was really trying to take that pressure and remove me from that role. The other issue really came down to trust. God was trying to get me to understand that as long as I put my trust in what I have, I would never be able to place my complete trust in Him.

> **SPIRITUAL TRUTH**: *Then the Lord said unto Moses, Behold I will rain bread from heaven for you; and the people shall go out and gather a certain rate every day, that I prove them, whether they walk in the law, or no. (vs.4) And Moses said, this shall be, when the Lord shall provide meat in the evening and bread in the morning. (vs.8) (Exodus 16:4 & 8)*

I would not give God a chance to demonstrate His power to provide. Although I was "saved," all my trust was not in Him, but was instead in what I could orchestrate in my own life. I was still making the calls and too afraid to let go and truly let God have complete control of my life.

But God was not done. I got the five thousand and spent it on living expenses. I still had no job, as I was too busy trying to train for football, and there was no more money to depend on.

God had me exactly where he wanted me now, because although I wanted to call someone else, there simply was no one else to call. This is when I had to go to Sonya and tell her where we were financially. I explained to her that in the next few months we were going to be broke, and I was going to need to get a job. Without any hesitation or judgment she immediately responded, "And so will I." Talk about the power of teamwork—that is what God was establishing in us! Although we definitely were not living a lavish life anymore, it was so much simpler. Much of that was because we opened our hearts to the possibilities of receiving God's grace and unmerited favor. Not three days after that discussion, we both got jobs that allowed me to continue to train and us to still spend time together, as well as go to church. I had to work on a third-shift job, which was quite humbling because most of the men that I worked with knew who I was. Going from tackling All-Pro running backs to moving boxes and driving a forklift in a warehouse gave me a whole new perspective on how God creates success in the game of life. He is more interested in us placing our trust and confidence in Him than in what we have. He wants us to realize that apart from Him we can do nothing, and nothing great can happen in our lives.

> **SPIRITUAL TRUTH:** *For promotion comes neither from the east, nor the west, nor from the south. As it is God who judges, He brings one down, and exalts (promotes) another. (Psalm 75:6)*

God was trying to teach me to place my total dependence and trust in Him and allow for there to be a spiritual divide between my past and the promise that rested in the future. To open myself up to greater miracles that He had planned. It is also when I realized that in order for us to receive power and promotion from the Lord, we must first be willing to relinquish it. Because until we do that the game of life will always be played out with us trying to make calls for God that He never intended for us to make.

CHAPTER 22

THE PROPHECY

NOW IN A NEW CITY, I was becoming very comfortable in the process of mentorship at our ministry. I could really see the value of being at the church. But deep down I really desired and wanted God to move on our behalf in regards to playing football. It was not my most important endeavor at this point, but I really did want to play again. As time passed, I became a bit anxious in the process of waiting for God to open a door of opportunity.

> **SPIRITUAL TRUTH:** *He who has the key of David, he who opens and no one shuts, and shuts and no one opens, I know your works. See, I have set before you an open door, and no one can shut it... (Revelation 3:7–8)*

Although my attitude for so many years had been about making my own decisions and playing the game of life based on my own rules and regulations, I was learning two dynamics of positive change. I did not have to play the game of life based on my own terms and strength. If I were going to change fully, embracing God's spiritual truth that rests in His word and wisdom is what would give me the best chance of winning in making the right calls in the game of life.

Although my original intent when we first moved to Charlotte was to continue playing in the NFL, that was not God's plan.

SPIRITUAL TRUTH: *"Many are the plans of a mans heart, but it is the Lord's purpose that shall prevail." (Proverbs 19:21)*

God's plan was for my wife and me to continue to come into the fullness of His knowledge and wisdom and to see life from His perspective instead of our own. We were able to gain this perspective through our experiences in the homeless ministry, serving in church, and being trained to teach others about the power that comes through the love of Jesus Christ.

Although my life was progressing, it was not as pleasant as it appeared, as there was a lot of pain and suffering. This felt somewhat like a "spiritual training camp" of sorts that was slowly teaching me how to play the game of life the right way. By this time I'd been through a year and eight months of spiritual training that felt like a long journey, but because of the level of accountability I was surrounded by, I was finally in a place of total surrender in regards to my faith in Jesus Christ. I still had fleshly battles of lust, thoughts about doing drugs and alcohol, and even feelings of frustration, but my patience was just better. However, the one thing that seemed to be on hold was my plan of playing in the NFL. It did not matter how much I prayed; it just was not happening.

I really started to get frustrated and take plans into my own hands by making phone calls to players, friends, and former teammates. I wanted an answer that would help me solve life's issues on my own. Typically, I would have really tried to make something happen, but the power of the Holy Spirit just would not let me.

One day in church it was my turn to serve on the usher team, so I had to be there early to pray and get ready for the congregation. I had a lot on my mind and really wanted to return to playing, not so much for monetary reasons but to take all that I had learned to help other players know that there was a better way to play the game of life. It was my turn to give back, and on that morning as we were praying I earnestly prayed to God, "I give football to you Lord, it does not belong to me, but you Lord, if you desire to take it away, then so be it, as my desire is to serve you and you alone." While praying this prayer, I started to cry, because what God was requiring was for me to let go of football and give it to Him. I was no longer going to hold it as a god in my life, so if I truly said in my heart that I loved and trusted Him I would not put anything before Him.

SPIRITUAL TRUTH: *You shall have no other gods before me. (Exodus 20:3)*

It was a time of real spiritual growth and commitment. My wife's and my hearts were fully engaged in the process of giving back and doing everything with the little we had to make a difference in the lives of those who did not have much. The crazy thing was that even in that process, I would still reflect back from time to time on how selfish I used to be and how far God had brought me. In fact, the closer I got to God, the less I focused on football.

After my prayer, our service started. It was a typical Sunday morning service and Pastor Barbara Cameron had just delivered a message during the offering about how important it was to give. How our lives must be open to the possibilities of the miracles that rest in the heart of the generous. Then she brought to the stage a guest speaker by the name of Sandra Appleberry. Now mind you, I had never met this lady before in my life, plus I was simply doing my normal usher job, escorting members of the church to their seats. As I sat a couple of the members down right at the beginning of service, Pastor Sandra, said, "Stop the music!" She looked directly at me and said, "You, come here!"

I said, "Me?"

She said, "Yes you!"

I wanted to ask for what, but I knew that whatever she had to say was of dire importance. She said, "Is that your wife?" and I said, "Yes ma'am." It was like she knew everything about me. She said, "Come here." We slowly walked up to the altar fearful, but with great anticipation, and as we got there, God began to speak through her.

She said. "I do not know what you do, but someone else's career is going sour for your good. I hear the Lord saying that if I could just get back some of the money I lost, I would do better."

It was at this moment that I broke spiritually, because I used to say that all the time. I knew the only way she could have known this is if God told her.

She continued, "The Lord told me to tell you within seven days there will be clarity and on the eighth day there will be a new beginning. I see you just leaping, dancing and praising God like never before as this time God has prepared you for something greater."

After she gave this prophetic word I literally did not know what to think. My mind was blown and I simply did not know what to do. How do you respond to a word so powerful, so timely, and so on point? I cried my eyes out for what seemed like an eternity. They were tears of joy, and I had no idea the affect this word would have on my life. But one thing for sure is that my wife and I needed to hear this word. We were at our breaking point. Although we were extremely at peace at where God had us, we really needed a financial breakthrough. We needed a glimpse of hope that God had our backs. This is exactly what this prophetic word did for us. It gave us the strength and wind under our sails to press forward.

Just as God had spoken so did He also move on our behalf. Within seven days the Jacksonville Jaguars called and brought me down for a workout. I was thinking, how does this happen? How does God know exactly when and where to speak to us, that will move us to new dimensions in our faith and hope in Him? This word was a game changer—it was the word we needed to hear. It gave us strength not only to move forward, but to also believe and expect that what Pastor Appleberry spoke would indeed come to past.

What did I learn the day this prophecy came? That God is no respecter of persons, and if you are crazy enough to hold onto your faith and trust him for the impossible, he will indeed open the doors that many thought were not possible.

SPIRITUAL TRUTH: *Faith without works is dead. James 2:14–26*

I had to travel to Jacksonville and they made it very clear that this was just a workout. Ten other linebackers joined me in the workout. I had not played a down of football in a year and eight months, so doubt naturally started to creep in, but

I remembered all the hard work I had done and just said to myself, "You got this."

I made up in my mind that my faith would match my works, and I was not going back home without a job. We began the workout, and not many minutes into it the coaches started sending players home. It was down to me and another guy, but God's prophetic word would shine through. The general manager came up to us and said, "You both had great workouts, but we need to see the status of the linebacker who has been injured, and if his injury is serious we will be signing one of you to a contract later today." I really did not want to hear another "no." I needed some good news, and although having the tryout was 110% better than what we had experienced in the last year and eight months, we really needed to experience God finish what He had started. I believed in my heart it was going to be done, but I hadn't signed a contract and, to be honest, I was worried it was not going to happen. It was at this moment that I remembered, "I can see you just leaping, dancing, and praising God like never before," and as I sat in the hotel room awaiting the call, I did just that. I started thanking and praising God for the contract, lifting up the name of Jesus and seeing that what seemed impossible becoming possible.

SPIRITUAL TRUTH: *Even God, who quickens the dead and calls those things that be not as though they were. (Romans 4:17")*

It was at that very moment, as I was experiencing the most intense praise I had within me, that the Jacksonville Jaguars called my phone and said, "Welcome to the Jaguar family!" I couldn't believe it was really happening. I had experienced so much bad news that although I knew this miracle was taking place, it was simply hard for me to believe.

It's at times like this when games are won and lost in life. At key moments when our backs are against the wall, when we have not experienced victory in a long time and we expect defeat, God comes along and sends the right word, at the right time, to shift our faith and hope to trust even in what we cannot see. These are the moments that are "Game Changers."

CHAPTER 23

THE POWER
OF FRIENDSHIP

SOMETIMES YOU MAY have friends who are only in your life for a temporary period of time. Most of the time you will not realize why they are there until they are gone. Sometimes that means having people in your life who will take advantage of you and abuse the relationship you may have with them. But then there are friends who will stick closer than a brother. This is what I learned about three men that God strategically placed in my life at keys moments that helped me realize the value and powerful gift of friendship. It can indeed be the most valuable asset that you can possess, or the most dangerous in regards to helping you reach God's desired destination for your life. Having the wrong friends can also present tremendous detours that can set you back so far that sometimes we cannot recover in the game of life.

SPIRITUAL TRUTH: *Do not make friends with a hot-tempered man, do not associate with one easily angered, or you may learn his ways and get yourself ensnared. (Proverbs 22:24–25)*

I have had to learn the hard way about having friends who were only in relationship with me to benefit themselves. But in this case the men that God had placed were brothers. While playing for the Jacksonville Jaguars, there was a key moment when I was injured and experiencing tremendous panic and duress from not knowing what the future would bring and how I was going to provide for my wife laid heavy on my mind. But my great friend, teammate, and brother Renaldo Wynn and his wife LaTonya were there helping guide us through the process, praying with my wife and me and being an encouragement to our souls. I mean, when you are part of a winning team but have become accustomed to losing, you really do not want to leave that environment. And even greater, when the people are great, it makes it that much better. But this day was not so great, because Jacksonville had given me some very bad news that they were going to release me and move in a new direction.

The news had come down from the front office. I was dejected. I walked down the hallway back to my locker and entered into the locker room, and the first person I saw was my brother and friend, Renaldo Wynn. I went right up to him and told him what had happened, and he looked me right in my eyes as only a brother could and said, "Brother, God has a plan. Do not be discouraged. My family and I will stand with you and yours."

This statement was powerful. This wasn't my first time being let go from a team, but this time not only were we winning on the field, but I was also winning in the game of life, walking with real men and women who had a heart for God and really desired to serve God with a whole heart.

> **SPIRITUAL TRUTH:** *And you my son Solomon, acknowledge the God of your father, and serve Him with wholehearted devotion and with a willing mind, for the Lord searches every heart and understands every desire and every thought. If you seek Him, he will be found by you, but if you forsake Him, He will reject you forever. (1 Chronicles 28:9)*

This was a whole new experience and attitude from those that we were walking with, and it truly made a huge difference on how we handled the incident.

My first time being released, the only encouragement I received was, "Good luck, man!"

When that happened, I thought to myself are you telling me that I was good enough hang out with, drink and do drugs, but now I'm only another player that was cut?

But Renaldo and the rest of my teammates really went beyond saying goodbye. They gave me a jolt of faith that encouraged my hope and caused me to have joy again. Even in the face of defeat, I still felt victory. This is what Renaldo and his family were able to give us, and it was the exact push we needed to trust God for the greater good.

God opened up another door of opportunity not many days later that challenged us to join our new team of the Washington Redskins. As I arrived in Washington, D.C., I really did not know what to expect except that I had to play well on the field and hopefully find some more brothers like I had in Jacksonville. I had learned from that experience that when you have the right teammates in the game of life, they will constantly encourage you to have a winning attitude, even in the face of adversity.

> **SPIRITUAL TRUTH**: *Two are better than one, because they have a good return for their work; If one falls down, his friend can help him up. But pity the man who falls and has no one to help him up! (Ecclesiastes 4:9–10 NIV)*

Although leaving the Jacksonville Jaguars and signing with the Redskins had been extremely difficult for my wife and me, it was turning out to be a tremendous blessing. God was moving us to a new place, and although I missed Renaldo and his family, what was really troubling me was whether I would meet another man like him.

It turns out it didn't take long, because just after I signed with the Redskins and was in the process of getting to know the organization and its people, I began to meet some of my new teammates. The first person I met was my new strength coach, Dan Riley, and my new workout partner, James Thrash. He was a tall, chiseled brother, whom I did not know from playing, nor did I know anything personally about him, but I immediately noticed that he was serious about his craft, training, and God. We were thrust into a relationship together, but even that was the hand of God.

The thing that was so funny was that linebackers usually didn't like working out with receivers, because they were the "pretty boys." But James was not even close to that, and I found that out the first day we worked out together when Dan Riley came to me and said, "They say you are a hard worker, so I was going to put you with one of our team's leaders and hard workers."

I was thinking, this guy is not going to be strong enough to train with me, but boy, was I wrong. That is exactly what we do in the game of life: we size people up, thinking we have them figured out based on a preconceived judgment that they will fit the mold that is in our minds. This is exactly how we miss the opportunity to have GREAT PEOPLE in our lives.

So in my heart, I had something to prove, never knowing at that point that God was placing us together and revealing to me that James was strong in his mind and body, but more importantly his faith. When it comes to the game of life, it is imperative that you have friends whose faith is just as strong, or stronger, than your own.

SPIRITUAL TRUTH: *As iron sharpens iron, so one man sharpens another. (Proverbs 27:17 NIV)*

James Thrash was the exact iron that God was using to sharpen me. It did not take long to realize that there was something unique in him. As I was still upset of the loss of my great friend and teammate in Renaldo Wynn, God was restoring what had been lost through James.

We sat down in the locker room to share a very intimate conversation. We could tell that we were kindred spirits and that God had prepared our hearts at a common place, which was our passionate faith in Jesus Christ. That made room for us to start pressing forward into real conversation about our past experiences, which is what true friendship is based on: finding that common ground and being honest and open about our experiences in the game of life.

James asked, "What is the most important thing to you?"

I responded, "God, my family, and my faith. Without that, I struggle."

James said, "I agree, but I cannot live without God's word."

We both were declaring our faith to one another, but more importantly to God. That tore down the pride that comes along with the game of football, where everything seems only surface because of the competition of winning jobs. James and I did not see each other in that way. We helped each other know who we were by being honest and by understanding why we were even with the Redskins and how we could grow together to become greater for God. It felt so good to know that God had given me a brother like him. It gave me the reassurance that I was not alone. Our relationship and friendship was not based on perception, but reality.

Now talk about being real—Troy Vincent was as real as they come. Troy and I first met off the playing field, but we found common ground in the game of life. We met at a Christian Athletes United for Spiritual Empowerment (CAUSE) Conference, and although I knew who he was as a football player, I had no idea who he was as a man. His credentials on the field spoke for themselves as an All-Pro cornerback for the Philadelphia Eagles. But what I would soon learn is that he was a devoted father, leader, and man of God who was committed to building men and families. A man cannot be judged solely for his behavior on the field. Even more than that is how we have all these preconceived notions about other people because of our own issues, and sometimes we never allow what we really need in terms of friendship to enter our lives. I was so thankful that I did not allow for the title of All-Pro Pro-Bowler get in the way of the man God was trying to reveal to me in Troy.

From early in my friendship with Troy, what I loved most about him was his authenticity. He was not worried about pleasing others or putting on this facade of making people see him in the public eye in one light and being a total different person in another. It really was a breath of fresh air because I honestly had been praying for God to send more men like him into my life. Not because I was being judgmental, but because I really needed people who were just "REAL" for a change. Renaldo, James, and now Troy gave me that. I had fought so long to put on this fake image so people would think one way about me, because the only value I thought I had was in the sport of football. But once I got around the right people who cared and were real and authentic, it truly helped me to see beyond the boundaries of the football field. I started looking at the game of life for what it really was through the eyes of God.

Then came that special moment in one of our men's breakout sessions at the conference when I was really able to see the value of why God was establishing a bond between Troy and I. From a football perspective, I felt inferior to him, although I never expressed it because of what we did have in common outside of playing football. He was a star player and I was a special teamer and back-up linebacker. So why would he even entertain the fact of embracing friendship? Boy, was I surprised to find out that the more I thought one thing was true, the more God would prove another. Many of the men were discussing their struggles with sin in the breakout session, but I was afraid to say I was going through the same thing.

Troy sat there silently watching and listening to all the men complaining like the Israelites about their struggles and their wives, and then in one instant, he turned to the crowd of athletes, and said, "How bad do you want out of it?"

Ironically, I was one of those men who had struggled with lust, sin, and fitting in for so many years, hoping God would come down from heaven and deliver me from this tough play I was facing in the game of life that, in all honesty, it was like making a mistake in a game. Instead of having a short-term memory and moving on to the next play, I would continue to dwell on that mistake, never being able to pull myself out of the mess. I just kept "replaying" one bad mistake after another, hoping for miracle and then finally reaching the point of no return and simply giving up and giving in.

But on this day Troy made the call of lifetime that would change the framework of how I saw and played the game of life. He challenged every man in that room—and trust me, there were future Hall of Fame guys in that room—to put our titles aside and for just once, "Be Real." He said boldly,

"We can sit here all day long talking about where we used to be or where we are now, but what are you going to do about it?"

There was a dead silence. All these men of valor, tough mindset, and build were brought to their knees of humility through one man's voice speaking a bold word of truth.

SPIRITUAL TRUTH: *So Paul and Barnabas spent considerable time there, speaking boldly for the Lord. (Acts 14:3)*

We were either going to reject the words spoken, or allow for their power to take full effect on our lives, because God was surely operating in that room that day. I knew one thing for sure, and for the rest of my life: I knew what a real friend was supposed to look like, what type of men I wanted and needed in my life, and that Troy Vincent would be my brother forever. Whether he wanted to be my friend or not, I was going to be his.

So how does this all relate to me and where I was with regard to friends I may have right now? God knows who we need and should be in our lives to help us carry out the right plays in the game of life so we can have the success we deserve to have. Although we have one picture of what and whom they should look like, we really need to get out of God's way and allow for Him to send the right people at the right time to press us higher toward Him.

Although all these men were uniquely different, Renaldo, James, and Troy all came at key moments in my life when everything was on the line and I had to make the call. God used each of them to help push me in the right direction. It was by God's design that these men had come into my life at just the right time. Renaldo came as an encourager of vision, James came as a strong support and tower to push me beyond my comfort zone, and Troy came as a strong tower of challenge as well as an example to bring about true change in my life. He really gave me a clear vision of God's expectation and standard for my life.

> **SPIRITUAL TRUTH:** *Now therefore put away your foreign gods that are among you and turn your hearts to the Lord, the God of Israel. Then the people promised Joshua, 'We will serve the Lord, our God, and will listen to His voice.' (Joshua 24: 23–24)*

Each one of these men encouraged me to go higher in God, and each encouraged me in a different area in the game of life. Life will be played out, but we all must choose what rules we are going to live by. God can send his word, great friendship, and examples to follow, but it will always be our choice to make the right or wrong call when it comes to our lives.

CHAPTER 24

EVEN IN DEATH GOD STILL PROVIDES LIFE

WE ALL KNOW that death is a part of life, but what do you do when it comes unexpectedly?

> **SPIRITUAL TRUTH**: *Otherwise, He would have needed to suffer often since the foundation of the world; but now once at the consummation of the ages He has been manifested to put away sin by the sacrifice of Himself. And inasmuch as it is appointed for men to die once and after this comes judgment, so Christ also, having been offered once to bear the sins of many, will appear a second time for salvation without reference to sin, to those who eagerly await Him. (Hebrews 9: 26–28)*

Sometimes death comes when you have had no time to prepare for the hurt, pain, and emotional fallout of losing someone who was so close to you. Dealing with the death of one person is one thing, but when you have to deal with two, it can literally devastate you and throw you into such an emotional whirlwind that sometimes you do not have any way to pull yourself out. Here I was in the prime of my career as a professional athlete. Sonya and I just had our second child. I had just spoken to the best man in my wedding, my best friend for life, and the man I called my brother. Ryan and I were so tight and shared this unique bond that was unbreakable. We could get on the phone for hours and talk about serious matters or issues that were just plain silly. I had just walked into the house after training, about to grab some late lunch at my kitchen table, when I got the call. Ryan's brother was on the other end, and he said, "Eddie, I have something to tell you."

By the tone of his voice, I knew something was wrong. I had experienced the same voice when I lost my older brother years before. I replied, "What is it, man?"

He said, "Ryan is gone, man!"

I couldn't believe it. "How could he be gone? I just spoke to him last week. Where did he go?" I spoke as if he were missing or had left to go somewhere, hoping that was the case.

But his brother immediately responded, "No, Eddie, he is dead!"

I broke emotionally and spiritually, and all these questions starting rolling through my mind: How? When? Where? Why? I immediately responded, "How did he die?"

Then the bomb dropped. "He took his own life. His son and I found him." In the midst of his voice cracking, my mind was racing at what seemed like a thousand miles an hour; I immediately went into crisis repair mode.

"How are you, brother, and how is Ryan's son? What's next step? What can I do?" I dropped every emotion I felt and focused on Ryan's immediate family, which was all I could do to keep my sanity after losing someone that close. I could not believe that I had just spoken with him but did not know there was something that bad in his life; that as close as we were, he could not talk to me about it. I started going over our conversation, trying to dissect every ounce of it to see if I missed something or if there was something I could have said or done to change his mind. I mean, this was my childhood best friend and friend for life. We were inseparable, no matter the distance or time. Feelings of guilt, anger, and resentment started to creep in. What was so bad? Why do this at this point in his life? We both made some bad plays in the game of life, but we were both also learning how to keep things in perspective and move forward. I kept playing the possibilities of what could have happened over and over in my head, until I had a quiet moment to realize this one thing: Some battles are not ours, but the Lord's.

SPIRITUAL TRUTH: *This is what the LORD says to you: 'Do not be afraid or discouraged because of*

this vast army. For the battle is not yours, but God's.'
(2 Chronicles 20:15)

This was neither a battle nor an opponent that I was equipped to beat. There was no winning or losing in this situation, but simply managing life. This trial and test had come to break me, by attacking someone who was closest to my heart.

God healed me from the hurt of my past, and I was finally starting to move pass it, but this emotional blow seemed to spiral me right back into a poor mindset. I played it off by trying to be the hero and savior of Ryan's family, contributing and doing everything I could in my limited power. On the outside I appeared strong, but the emotional trauma and torture I felt mentally was truly getting the best of me.

As I battled out of this, an early-morning call came from Kevin's wife. Time stood still as I picked up the phone. I heard her voice say, "Eddie, your brother is gone." I said again, "Gone where? How? When? What happened?"

She said, "The medics tried to save him, but his body just would not respond. They say he had a heart attack in his sleep."

These two incidents were so much the same, as they had both occurred at pivotal moments and times in the game of life. In one instance, I became very angry with God, and in the other because of my perspective, faith, and hope in God, the process of healing and deliverance was a lot easier. Although

Ryan's death was extremely difficult, it helped prepare me for Kevin's. They both were very traumatic, as Kevin and I had become so close that I considered his family my own family. We spent years playing together, retired together and transitioned out of the game of football together. We shared a special bond of friendship that, for me, went beyond the field, affecting who I was as a man. To have lost him in such an untimely manner broke my heart not only for him but also for his wife, who was pregnant, and the two children they had together. It was pain that I personally experienced and a pain I had for his wife, as what I was feeling could not compare to what she was going through.

What could I do? There was nothing I could do for her or her children, except be there in whatever way I could.

But then there came this realization that the scares from both of these untimely deaths had severely taken a toll on me emotionally. As I often did, I buried the emotion and disengaged from the process of dealing with the actual pain. I would start to feel depressed and cast it off as if it were nothing, just as I had done so many times before. I started eating a lot and became emotionally detached, and, without telling anyone, secretly started drinking again. I kept acting as if everything was okay, but I was reeling on the inside. I could not show weakness, even though I had learned years ago that this was the exact opposite of what I needed to do. God had already taught me that in order to be strong in Him, I must first be willing to be vulnerable to show my weakness.

Eventually I reached 265 pounds, and it was then, when I was depressed and broken, that God came to meet me again. I was in a park, sitting in my truck, crying and thinking about taking my own life. I heard God say so clearly, "This is not your path, son. Get up and move quickly, for I have much work for you to do. Your season is not yet come, as I am taking you to a greater place in me. Although the journey will not be easy, I will provide everything you need to carry out the assignment. Do not haste, as I shall be with you."

Time stood still in this moment, because for the first time I knew that even through all the abuse from my dad and the drugs, alcohol, womanizing, dealing with rejection, life transition, and depression, God still had a plan for me. The pain was simply part of the process to birth God's purpose. I was spending so much time focusing on the pain that I was missing the process of being positive within the purpose of God's plan for my life. The words God spoke to me that day gave me hope to press forward to a greater place in him; to not see life through the eyes of sorrow and guilt, but through grace.

> **SPIRITUAL TRUTH**: *I was the door; if anyone enters through Me, he will be saved, and will go in and out and find pasture. The thief comes only to steal and kill*

and destroy; I came that they may have life, and have it abundantly. I was the good shepherd; the good shepherd lays down His life for the sheep. (John 10:10)

The enemy wanted to use both Ryan's and Kevin's deaths as a way to make me so depressed that I would lose myself in the process. The bond I shared with these men was still not broken spiritually, but I was no longer broken anymore by the grace of God.

SPIRITUAL TRUTH: *When we were controlled by our old nature, sinful desires were at work within us, and the law aroused these evil desires that produced a harvest of sinful deeds, resulting in death. But now we have been released from the law, for we died to it and are no longer captive to its power. Now we can serve God, not in the old way of obeying the letter of the law, but in the new way of living in the Spirit. (Romans 7:5-7)*

I no longer had to live bound to this sin nature that constantly tried to tell me I could not make it; I could not be healed, or I had no more strength. Instead, the power of God's spirit gave me strength in the midst of a broken mindset and heart to stand, still proclaiming the victory that lived through the work of the cross that Jesus bore on Calvary. It was a defining moment of my faith to realize that even in death, God can still provide life.

CHAPTER 25

NO MORE SECRETS

ALTHOUGH MY LIFE, for the most part, was going well, complacency started to creep back in. I had great friendships, but the one thing about friendship is that you can't have great friends without having a level of trust and accountability to share all facets of your life. Not to share is to leave an open door for the enemy to come in.

> **SPIRITUAL TRUTH:** *"And do not give the devil a foothold." Ephesians 4:27*

Life can present so many distractions that cause us to lose focus on our purpose: Living a life for God and walking in integrity. When we become distracted, we can repeat the mistakes of our past. Just like in sports, when you make one mistake and do not address it, it will lead to more mistakes that could eventually cost you in the game of life. We have the ability to succeed, but we are too busy living life as a three-ring circus act, juggling all kinds of emotional, spiritual, physical, and mental roles in the bigger game of life. This lifestyle can really wind up costing us.

We can lose ourselves in life and forget who we are, not intentionally, but because we lose focus of who we are. We lose sight of why and what we are supposed to be doing. We start molding ourselves to fit the environments and people we are around to make ourselves feel good.

> **SPIRITUAL TRUTH**: *Do not conform to this world, but be transformed, by the renewing of your mind. Then you will be able to test and approve what God's will is—his good, pleasing, and perfect will. (Romans 12:2)*

How many times have we conformed and transformed ourselves into something we really aren't? How many times have we had every good intention of being great for God and yet somehow lost ourselves at key moments in life? God calls us higher, yet out of convenience and to be appealing to man, we lose ourselves and, ultimately, the game we are playing. Instead of stopping and refocusing on what is most important, we wind up struggling and giving in to the temptations and battles we are confronted with.

This is exactly what happened when I fell to the temptation of a young lady. How does a man who is a devoted father, mentor, leader, and servant in the church go from having everything to being distracted by a woman? I had a beautiful wife who loved me, and a wonderful family and great friends, but something inside me was empty. I was in a grocery store, of all places, and made eye contact with a young lady who was extremely attractive. Nothing new to me, as I had seen plenty of gorgeous women throughout my life and not been moved by their beauty. But for whatever reason, because of how busy my life was, I had truly lost who I was. I was not as consistent in my prayer life, was not in church, had really not been opening up to my wife intimately, nor was I giving way to any accountability in my life. Here I was in this grocery store, making eye contact with her.

My gut said, "Leave it alone, don't go down this path. You are past this place—keep moving." But I had a burning desire that just would not let this go.

I did not feel lust or long for sex; instead, I loved the feeling of this woman "paying me attention"—I mean, really having an eye for me. It made me feel desired and excited again, something I had not felt in a long time in my marriage. I wanted to feel it, but because I was "too busy providing," that glance turned into a gaze and a gaze into an introduction to a path that would come with a heavy price.

I pushed my cart in her direction and was too afraid to say anything, so I just kept walking. I so wanted to ask for her name, but I had a very strong conviction, so I let it go and kept shopping. By the time I had paid for my items the feeling had subsided, as it had many times before, but as I was loading my car she walked by, and our eyes met again.

> **SPIRITUAL TRUTH:** *At the window of my house I looked down through my lattice, I saw among the simple, I noticed the young men, a youth who had no sense. He was going down to the street near her corner, ...then came a woman to meet him, dressed in revealing clothing, with crafty intent. (Proverbs 7: 6,7 & 10)*

At this point I did not say anything, but I made a decision spiritually and mentally to let my guard down. I got into my car and started to pull out and instead of just waving bye, I slowed down and stopped.

I asked her, "What is your name?"

She responded with a very calm voice as if to reassure me everything was fine. I relaxed and told her my name and asked for her number. She gave it to me, and I responded, "I'll call you, okay?"

She said, "You'd better, because I think you're gorgeous!"

I was like, *oh my God* on the inside.

I was still longing to be someone who was wanted. My mom had played that role for a part of my life, then girlfriends at another time, and then my wife for a while, and now I was opening my life up to a woman I did not know. I had longed to be affirmed, for someone of the opposite sex to tell me how and what they thought about me. The bigger issue was not the affirmation, but my insecurity and lack of understanding of who I was in God. It made me question my God-given ability and seek to be affirmed by people instead of being affirmed by God. I had it all wrong.

SPIRITUAL TRUTH: *Therefore let not anyone who thinks he stands take heed, lest he fall. (1 Corinthians 10:12)*

How did I get here? My life was in order. I had everything I could desire: a great wife, beautiful family, and good job. It all was perfect on the outside, but on the inside I was an absolute mess. This little boy was crying out for attention that in reality only God could fulfill. It had taken me all these years to realize that "NO WOMAN" could ever replace the affirmation of being credited as worthy in the eyes of God, and that worthiness was not based on how great I was, but how great He is. All these years I had been reacting to all the hurt of feeling that my dad did not love me and had rejected me, seeing the abuse of my mother, not being in touch with my emotions to talk my feelings out, being on the defensive, not trusting, being fearful, and using my size and bravado as a means to express myself to people through the image I had built up through the game. It had finally caught up with me. I was so busy looking for love in the wrong places that I was unable to face the truth that literally was right in front of me daily. So I kept dragging myself down this road of infidelity and deceit that eventually caught up to me the day my wife finally figured out that the text messages were not from my buddies but from a woman who had captivated my mind and spirit. In my spirit, I did not want to continue this relationship outside of my marriage, but the longing of wanting to feel loved and desired cried louder within my soul. Even though on the outside I had this way of presenting myself to the crowd, inside I was this lonely, depressed, pathetic example of a man. I did not even know how to love myself, let alone my wife, family, and children.

> **SPIRITUAL TRUTH**: *I do not understand what I do. For what I want to do, I do not do, but what I hate to do, I do. (Romans 7:15)*

I desired to do what was right, but it would take me hitting rock bottom the day my wife finally figured out what was going on. She found a text message that said, "When can we meet again?"

She didn't address it immediately but instead held onto it as if to wait for the right moment. I got home from work and she was in the bedroom with the lights dimmed. I could feel the tension in the room as she sat upright on the bed. I knew without her saying a word that I was done.

Sonya said, "Eddie, I need to talk to you."

When those words came out of her mouth I knew it was over. I said "About what?"

She said, "I think you know about what. Eddie, I was going to give you one chance and one chance only to tell me the truth, and if I find out you are not, we are done." Those words cut through me like a knife. It was as if God himself was speaking to me through her, as if God were saying, "You cannot run from yourself any longer, Eddie. It is time to face who you really are."

Knowing I could not keep this secret any longer, I answered, "Sonya, if you are talking about the text message, it is true and I have not been faithful toward you or our children."

The look of dismay and disappointment on her face broke my spirit and made me feel like the worst loser ever. Never did I desire to be unfaithful to my wife and family, but the narcissistic attitude, pride, and selfishness that I had learned to ignore had fooled me into thinking I could have my cake and eat it too.

When you are looking for others to make you feel good about yourself and feel affirmed, you are doomed to repeat the mistakes of your past and never come to a real place of being comfortable in who God created you to be.

I told Sonya everything, and I felt like a weight had lifted. For so long I had lived this lie: from drugs and alcohol, to womanizing, to being unfaithful, to being insecure, to being afraid to trust and ultimately having people in my life to tell me what I wanted to hear, instead of receiving the truth of what I needed to hear. I had accepted rejecting the truth for lies and deceit, but this time God was not allowing me to make another play until I could deal with the bad ones that were right in front of me.

God had allowed me to hit bottom, and I had no other choice but to look up and start working myself back to the top. But that would not come without me making some real life decisions about my commitment to repairing all that had been lost in my relationship with God, my wife, my children, my spiritual family as a whole, and all the people I had hurt along the way.

I was in the game of my life, and losing was not an option. I made some serious personal fouls that I was going to have to recover from, but I made a decision in my heart that I was going to get it right this time around. I was not going to allow the grace that God was extending to me be another means to patch up the problems in my personal life. I seriously was going to allow for God's grace to heal me this time, both because of my commitment to receive it and also because I understood the price it took to give it.

CHAPTER 26

COMMITMENT TO BEING ACCOUNTABLE

SONYA AND I started out with two commitments. The first was to create spiritual, mental, and emotional boundaries and actively engage the process of realizing that I truly had a problem with the image of who I was. The second and most necessary commitment was to open our lives to spiritual accountability.

> **SPIRITUAL TRUTH:** *Therefore, confess your sins to one another and pray for one another, that you may be healed. The prayer of a righteous person has great power as it is working. (James 5:16)*

If our relationship was going to be restored and healed, I was going to have to embrace the right coaching this time. The crazy thing is, because I had played sports my whole life, I knew what it meant to make a good play and when to make a bad one. The only way you improve from your mistakes is to take some serious time of reflection and commit to the process of true change, with a desire to get better, leaving success as your only option.

> **SPIRITUAL TRUTH:** *Do not be afraid or discouraged, for the Lord will personally go ahead of you. He will be with you; he will neither fail you nor abandon you. (Deuteronomy 31:8)*

The first call we made together was to share the intimate story with someone who we knew was spiritually mature enough to deal with the harsh reality of this fallout in our lives, someone who could objectively look through the muck and mire and speak life into dead and dry places. As I shared this terrible nightmare of a story with my wife, she looked me dead in my eyes and said, "If we're going to do this, you're going to have to tell Pastor Mitchell."

I thought, crap, not Pastor Mitchell. I loved and respected him so much as a spiritual father and mentor that I did not want to disappoint him.

How could I share this with him? I looked back at Sonya and said, "I will do it, and I mean it," although in my gut I really didn't mean it, not because I was trying to keep hiding, but because I really was ashamed and did not want to disappoint my spiritual mom and dad.

I immediately called Pastor and asked him if my wife and I could meet with him about something very serious. He said, "Of course, son."

When he said these words, it felt like the same day that Tony Dungy had looked me in my eyes and said, "Eddie, you are a better man than this, son."

When Pastor said, "Of course, son," it was a term of endearment, expressing love and trust. I had betrayed that trust with him, my wife, children, spiritual family, and most importantly, God.

The day to meet with him came. It felt like my stomach was in my throat. I felt like I did right before I walked out of that tunnel to go and play football, except instead of having butterflies because of excitement and confidence to play a game, I had nervous energy and fear of telling Pastor the truth.

How would he respond? Would he reject me like my dad did? Could he trust me again? My mind was racing as we walked into the church. Here I was, a 230-pound outside linebacker who was accustomed to handling adversity and dealing with tough situations, but this time I would rather have quit and given in to the opposition than press forward. But there was no turning back. We entered Pastor's office, and he immediately said, "Let's go downstairs." So we walked downstairs into a very quiet room. That walk felt like an eternity.

We sat down and Pastor said, "So how are you guys doing?"

I looked at Sonya, as if to say, "Are you going to tell him?" She looked back at me as if to say, "You got us into this mess, you are going to own this to help get us out."

I cleared my throat and apprehensively began to share the story with this man I loved and respected. Pastor never wavered in his stern and honest approach. After I finished telling my story, he looked at me and said, "Eddie, are we at the bottom?"

I said, "Yes sir, we are at the bottom. Sir, I was at the bottom."

> **SPIRITUAL TRUTH:** *The hand of the Lord was upon me, and he brought me out by the Spirit of the Lord and set me in the middle of the valley; it was full of bones. He led me back and forth among them, and I saw a great many bones on the floor of the valley, bones that were very dry. He asked me, 'Son, of man, can these bones live?'*

I was at a crossroads in my life, and God was ready to restore what was dead, dry, and brittle and had produced so much bitterness. But it was going to take a tremendous commitment greater than myself to see that there was still hope of living again.

Pastor said, "Then we are ready to start working ourselves back up to the top." He paused for a moment and said, "Eddie, I see you as a man of many spiritual gifts, but your greatest weakness is your unguarded strength. You are like a man who has filled his 'life bag' with everything under the sun that the world has to offer, yet nothing could fill it because you have always had a leaking hole in your bag. No matter what you tried to fill it with, it would never have been enough."

As he spoke these wise, stern, and prophetic words, I broke emotionally. It was the first time in my life where God was saying to me, "You have run long enough, and I am not going to allow you to run anymore." All these years I tried to fill the void in my heart that started the day I saw my dad beat my mother to the day we had to move in with my grandparents. All of those years I hid my emotions; instead of facing them, I coped by sabotaging myself and masking all my pain through the spirit of pride. In sports, pride was my strength, but in life it was my greatest weakness.

My wife then shared her pain and expectations and what she needed to move forward: counseling, setting up boundaries, and meeting with Pastor on a regular basis to establish a greater sense of accountability. She said, "I will not even consider this journey if these things are not put into place."

So Pastor asked, "Eddie, do you hear what she needs?"

I said, "Yes sir."

"No, do you really hear what she needs? She needs a sound commitment and real accountability that says you are not living a life apart from your family, but are a man who is engaged in the process of ensuring success spiritually, mentally, and emotionally."

It seemed like I was genuine, but how could I know for sure? For so many years I had kept secrets about my emotions, drugs and alcohol, or women I was attracted to. So Pastor sat up in his seat and said, "Eddie, your life is no longer your own. You belong to God!" He consoled Sonya and assured her that he would be with us through this process, no matter how long it took. He was our anchor and gave us the confidence to know that God was with us. Although we had what seemed like a huge appointment, to be honest, I was not sure we could defeat. This is where I had to put all pride aside. In the game of football, we are taught to never give in, work hard, and show strength, not weakness. But God was establishing a new way that required complete humility and debasement of self. Christ had set the example for me to follow, and for so long I had rejected it.

> **SPIRITUAL TRUTH:** *Who being in very nature God, did not consider equality with God something to be used to his own advantage, rather, he made himself nothing by taking the very nature of a servant being in human likeness, and being found in appearance as a man, he humbled himself by becoming obedient to death - even death on the cross! (Philippians 2:6)*

If I was going to win this game that was being played out, it would not be on my terms any longer, but His. I was all out of options. I had to humble myself and embrace the accountability that God was establishing in my life. I had never really embraced that level of openness to allow another man to speak about my life and know everything about me. It really was time to get real, because up until this point I was a fake.

My days of being selfish and making life all about me were over. I had been taught in the game of football that in order to succeed, you must always prepare for the worst, but expect the best. I had to tap into my spiritual reserves to know and believe that what had been spoken over my life through Pastor Mitchell would give me the ability to begin making the right calls in the game of life.

CHAPTER 27

THE DREAM TEAM

IT IS AMAZING how God sends the right people at just the right time to get you headed in the right direction so you can start playing the game of life God's way. Right after confiding the whole truth to my wife and Pastor Mitchell, I started to put in work, just like in the game of football. It was time to shift my mindset into game mode and stop taking my family and the people God had placed in my life for granted. How many times have we all been in situations in our lives where we have to make the call and we are either selfish and choose the wrong path, or we just don't know what to do? That kind of behavior is exactly what got me into the mess in the first place. In the sport of football there are owners, general managers, coaches, coaches assistants, proven systems and structures in place to hold us accountable, for the exact purpose of bringing the best out of us, to put us in position to have great success on the field and in life.

Being a player in the National Football League requires having people in your life you have to answer to, or you simply will not get better. But sometimes because of our past failures, bad relationships, broken trusts, and broken hearts, we start to develop a callus on our hearts disallowing the right people God is trying to get in our lives to come in.

> **SPIRITUAL TRUTH:** *For this people's heart has become calloused; they hardly hear with their ears, and they have closed their eyes. Otherwise they might see with their eyes, hear with their ears. (Matthew 13:15)*

Instead, we would rather try to play the game of life on our own, making all the calls as if we know exactly what to do in every circumstance or situation without ever seeking out those "life coaches and guardians" who can help us not go down paths that are no good for us.

A part of the biggest issue is realizing that the game film of our lives that is playing out is just not a good product. If there is a flaw in your game, then you have to recognize that it is your responsibility to realize that what you are doing is not working. You must have a heart that has a willingness to change and embrace the accountability necessary to put you in position to start winning more in life than you are losing. This is where the big problem comes in for men, because we have this hormone called testosterone running through our system. We believe that when something is broken we can fix it on our own, when in reality that is furthest from the truth. We sometimes would rather win in the game of life 20 times, getting all kinds of bruises, scrapes, strains, and sprains, instead of going to someone and simply saying, my life is "jacked up" and I need help.

> **SPIRITUAL TRUTH**: *Then He taught me, and He said to me, Take hold of my words with all your heart; keep my commands, and you will live. (Proverbs 4:4)*

But that requires too much work, and that would mean letting other men who are wiser and have more experience spiritually, mentally, emotionally, and even financially help guide us down the right path. This is exactly what I had to do. Enter the "Dream Team," which consisted of Pastor Chester L Mitchell, Pastor Chad Carlton, and Dr. Craig Mormon. Each of these men played a significant role in helping my wife and I heal from the hurt and brokenness I had exposed my family to, but more than that, they taught me how to embrace three things:

+ The power that rests in having sound boundaries.

+ The power of accountability.

+ The power of asking the most important question in life: Is it wise?

Pastor Mitchell was the key God used to unlock the door of mistrust that was in my heart, which had existed from the time I was little playing in the backyard with my Tonka truck. The abuse, mistrust, and brokenness I had seen as a child had become my standard for how I dealt with people and the game of life as a whole.

> **SPIRITUAL TRUTH:** *"Keeping mercy for thousands, forgiving iniquity and transgression and sin, and that will by no means clear the guilty; visiting (punishing) the iniquity of the fathers upon the children, and upon the children's children, unto the third and to the fourth generation. (Exodus 34:7)*

Pastor Mitchell helped me to see myself for where I really was, and not where I thought I was. He took the callus off my eyes and heart and helped me to embrace the power that rests in Godly accountability.

Most of us would ask, well what does this look like and why do I need that? I mean, we are all smart and driven people who know how to work through adversity, right? If that is indeed the case, then the bigger question is how do we get to places in our lives where we are not living up to God's standard? The reason is, until we allow for other people to know everything about who, what, and why we are who we are, true change can never happen.

We will play the game of life out with a sideline mentality, and instead of doing everything it takes to be great in life, we will sit on the sidelines, hoping to one day make a great play while bad ones play out one after another in the game of life. We must learn to embrace those spiritual leaders who are not our friends, but our mentors; otherwise, we risk history repeating itself. We all need a Pastor Mitchell, someone who knows our highest high and our lowest low in all facets of our lives. We can leave no stone unturned when we are committed to true change.

Then came Pastor Chad Carlton who, to be honest, was indeed my daily iron. He would ask me the tough questions face to face such as where I was in my life, how my wife and I were doing, and whether I was struggling in any area. Pastor Mitchell was teaching me the power of true accountability, and Pastor Chad was a huge complement, as he was the one who would hold me to the fire. He would continue to help give me a different perspective and encouraging me to embrace wisdom—not only embrace it, but apply it by putting the facts out there. He posed the hard questions, such as is this person good for your life; are they tearing your life down, or building it up? They are not going to do both. Most importantly, do you really need them right now? These questions were not there to control my life, but to help me grow and mature.

Dr. Craig Mormon was the glue; he was able to take all the mental, physical, emotional, and spiritual brokenness and put it all together again.

> **SPIRITUAL TRUTH:** *The sacrifices of God are a broken spirit; a broken and a contrite heart, O God, You will not despise. (Psalm 51:17)*

I had no time to make assumptions, acting as if what was broken was already fixed. I needed to do a lot of work alongside with my wife, family, and friends. It wasn't just about praying, worshipping, and fasting; I also had to deal with the hurt that I caused, while dealing with the hurt that existed in my heart. It started with where I was, and the first thing Dr. Craig Mormon submitted as an "uncompromisable option" was that boundaries must be put up. I was so used to dealing with people with such a big heart that one of my greatest fears was being rejected and telling people "no." Once I made a mistake I would rather stay in the mess instead of "rejecting them" or "being rejected." I know how much rejection hurts, because that is what I felt when I was five years old, thinking my dad did not love me and that he did not want me.

So I put this huge wall up in the form of drugs, sex, alcohol, women, and failed relationships, hoping that one of them would give me the answer. The other component to my brokenness was the fact that I had no boundaries in my life.

If you look at a football field, you will see white lines that differentiate between where the game is actually supposed to be played and the game that is out of bounds; emotionally and spiritually, I was doing both. Dr. Mormon taught me how to re-establish the boundaries in the game of life again. He taught me the value of saying "No" to people, which seems very easy but is not when you have a heart of compassion for people, and when every good intention, although it seems well, can really wind up coming back to hurt you. It was work, as this was not an overnight process, but a daily one, and sometimes a minute by minute, or as we refer to it in the sports world a "play-by-play" view.

So you have heard what a callus over the heart and eyes can do to you, but what are you willing to do about it? What changes are you willing to put into place to help you start winning in the game of life? Are you ready yet to look yourself in the mirror and ask this question: is Is what I am doing wise? It is necessary that you have a team that reignites the dream that God desires to birth in your life, to embrace the challenge that comes along with true change in order to become the man or woman that God has called you to be. A part of those things is understanding the importance of establishing boundaries and having a willingness to take that next step in allowing God to change your heart from one that is stony to one that is flesh.

SPIRITUAL TRUTH: *24For I will take you out of the nations; I will gather you from all the countries and bring you back into your own land. 25I will sprinkle clean water on you, and you will be clean; I will cleanse you from all your impurities and from all your idols. 26I will give you a new heart and put a new spirit in you; I will remove from you your heart of stone and give you a heart of flesh. 27And I will put my Spirit in you and move you to follow my decrees and be careful to keep my laws. Therefore you will be my people and I will be your God. (Ezekiel 36: 24–27)*

So here is the call: the Lord is always ready to do new things in our lives, but the greater question is, are we ready? Are we ready to embrace the change that is required, not out of necessity or compulsion, but because it is in us to see that we need it? Are we ready and willing to own whatever it takes to be great in God and in the game of life? Are we ready, not for some football, but to start changing from the inside out? We all have a choice to play the game of life either on the field within the rules or outside the lines of life, where we keep making one foul play after another. Ultimately it is our call. What's next?

CHAPTER 28

THE NEW YOU

ONE OF THE HARDEST THINGS to do in life is change how you think, because most of the decisions that we make are by-products of routines and habits we have formed over time through experiences in the game of life. Or they are reflections of hurt and pain we have experienced over time that now hold us captive and unable to see ourselves beyond where we may currently be. The problem with this is that if we do not position ourselves around the right people and environment, we risk continuing to live a life based on the perspective of our past instead of the promise that lives within the future. To do this requires a conscious, invested, and committed decision to allow God the authority to show us the "new you" He desires for us to become.

> **SPIRITUAL TRUTH:** *Therefore if any man be in Christ, he is a new creature: old things are passed away; behold, all things are become new. (2 Corinthians 5:17 KJV)*

But how? How do we become new? The way we become new is to stop thinking with a limited perspective of who we are in the game of life. Our attitude and perspective can determine what happens in the game of life before it is even played out. Because of our perspective, many of us cannot even believe in our potential, since we do not trust that it is even possible to be what and who God is calling us to.

In the sport of football we call it the mental edge, the belief that any time God gives us an opportunity, regardless of the arena in life, we cannot be beat. Is this arrogance? No, it is purely a belief that when we activate our faith in who we are in God it does not allow fear, doubt, or unbelief to quench the hope that rests in the assured confidence of God's word, His Holy Spirit's power, and the ability that He placed upon our lives.

There is not one of us who should ever think that anything great happens apart from God and because of our power. We miss the sovereignty of God's hand to show us who we really are in Him. We get stuck on what we can see with our own eyes, instead of allowing God to show us who we are through His.

Think about it: How does God take a former NFL player who was an addict, alcoholic, womanizer, adulterer, prideful, arrogant and unwise man, and inspire Him to allow the very weaknesses of his life to become strengths? We all know or have felt this feeling of inferiority that we are unworthy and that God cannot use us because of some bad calls we made in the game of life.

SPIRITUAL TRUTH: *There is therefore now no condemnation for those who are in Christ Jesus. (Romans 8:1)*

We would rather condemn ourselves over the problems that life has presented instead of the promises that are ever-present through God's grace. When really all we have to do is realize on a personal level, the only thing that is good in us is God. Everyone has a story, everyone has a past, and the good news is we all have a future. God desires to have His hands in all of it, if we will allow Him.

The problem is sometimes because we desire to have control over our lives and not allow for God to call the plays, we continue to make the same mistakes over and over instead of giving God a chance to reveal himself through His word in prayer, or to allow other men and women who have figured out the right way to play the game of life God's way. We expect to stay in the same position and posture of defeat when God's expectation is for us to change. Not only to change, but to become the "new creation" that He desires.

Sooner or later, we all hit bottom. I got a call from one of the young men I was mentoring, and he said, "Coach, I have something to tell you."

I had just finished up a training session with one of my clients in the gym, and music was blasting in the background. I said, "Hold on, man, let me get to a place where I can hear you." There was a moment of silence as I walked to my office.

"Okay, what's up, son?" I refer to a lot of the men God places in my life as "son" because I recognized early on that even as I did not have a father, many men need father figures. This is especially true when it comes to having someone to turn to when the game of life has gotten really tough and it feels like there is nowhere else to turn to for help.

He responded, "I got this girl pregnant." Now mind you, before he even went to school on a full scholarship I told him, "Whatever you do, do not engage yourself or become overly consumed with girls, as your focus should be on your faith, academics, and football."

> **SPIRITUAL TRUTH**: *Let your eyes look direct-*
> *ly forward, and your gaze be straight before you.*
> *(Proverbs 4:25)*

When he told me the news, I was a little upset, but isn't it amazing how the things we go through personally play out in the purpose of who and what God allows for us to experience. I respond, "How is the young lady doing with all of this?"

He said, "We are both okay with it. She has a good support system."

"You have to do what is right by her and this child, and you have created more stress in your life than you need to, but God will see you both through this, as long as you keep your eyes on God." Then I asked the big question: "Do you think you are ready to be a father?"

"No, but I don't have a choice now."

These are always powerful moments when the calls we make in life limit the amount of choices we have, regardless of whether they are positive or negative. Calls in the game of life are the key determining factor that sets limits in our lives, because they take every choice away.

"Have you talked to your head football coach yet?"

He said, "No."

"You have to do that, because if there is to be any success, you have to ensure that all players that are involved in the greater game of life understand where you are so that they can support you. Start with your positional coach since you already have a great relationship with him." Now mind you when I was facing this big call, I did not allow myself the openness to be coached. This young man did.

I told him, "You have to maintain great focus and faith now, son, as you cannot allow for this one bad play to affect the rest of your life. Now is time to prepare and wrap your mind around the reality of what has happened. Embrace the truth of it, and set a course to change who you are spiritually and personally. Then ensure that you take responsibility for what lies ahead."

He was very quiet, but I could tell that he was discouraged because of the tone of his voice. I said, "Son, you remember I shared my story with you many years ago in regards to my life, and how I have already walked where you are trying to go. I have had to make that tough call, where I, too, got someone pregnant. Instead of owning the responsibility, I chose the cowardly route. You do not have to. Use what seems to be bad and allow God to turn it around for your good."

He said, "Thank you so much, coach."

I told him, "I love you and am proud of the fact that you are being a man about this, and I will be with you every step of the way."

This situation teaches us that even sometimes when we have been coached to do right, we still choose to do wrong. Why do we do that? We have to hit rock bottom, hitting our heads on one bad mistake after another, choosing to call plays on our own when we know we are not qualified to, expecting God to deliver us once we are knee-deep in stress, worry, and fear. We try our best to sort life out, but never truly figuring it out. If we would just get out of our own way and allow God to have His way, we could truly find the identity, purpose, and plan He has for us. Much of the problem with that situation is more about the standard we set for our lives than the mistakes we make.

We start to glorify our problem and minimize the fact that God is greater than anything we could ever face, but even more than that—even in our most perfect moment in the game of life, we are still imperfect in the eyes of God. This is why we must choose to make a sound commitment to stop looking back at who we were or what has happened to us. We must allow for God to use us based on the experiences of our past, not living in them. I did not want this young man to live in the circumstance of where he was, but the promise of who God had called him to be. In order to do that we all must allow ourselves the chance to see ourselves as new. This is why we must stop wrestling with insecurity, as insecurity can take a person who is destined for greatness and deflate their entire framework of who they are. It steals our confidence in ourselves.

We all have to allow God to meet us where we are, not where we think we are in the fullness of His power. We have to allow Him to show us that if we are truly going to become new, it is going to take us putting down the thoughts of what we couldn't do, and start embracing the possibilities of what we can. It takes us working on things that bring about true change, like a self-discovery list:

+ Who am I?

+ Reading God's word daily.

+ Making that commitment of devotion.

+ Taking time to reflect over our lives on a spiritual, personal and emotional level.

+ Using the bad calls of our past to impact our future in a positive way.

+ Opening our hearts to be washed completely by God's word and the Holy Spirit's directives.

This is what helps us become new, but more importantly sets us up to make the right calls in the game of life so we are not always making halftime adjustments to the mistakes we make, but walking in the liberty and freedom of the promise that rests in God's plan and purpose for our lives.

CHAPTER 29

RAISING THE STANDARD

AT THE END OF THE DAY, regardless of how well we do in the game of life, God still expects us to continue to grow and raise the standard. Much of the standard is about our own personal, mental, emotional, and spiritual development, but the greater purpose is in being an example for others. It is about taking our lives, learning from many of the bad calls we have made, and seeking out game plans to show us how to play it better.

SPIRITUAL TRUTH: *And we all, who with unveiled faces contemplate the Lord's glory, are being transformed into His image with ever-increasing glory, which comes from the Lord, who is Spirit. (2 Corinthians 3:18)*

Much of the process of gaining ground on the opposition we face in the game of life is having a willingness to take a closer look at where we really are and to grab hold of the standard that has been set by God. We always have a tendency in life to go back to what we know, but that never gives us a winning opportunity when what we are competing against are old mindsets, generational curses, attitudes, and hopelessness that oftentimes rest in our hearts.

The only way to combat against this tendency is to ensure that there is a commitment to keeping God and His word as the true example that we set to call all the plays we may face in the game of life. What I learned is that man sets one standard, but God has His own. His way of doing things far supersedes anything we could ever imagine.

One day my wife and I picked up some food from the mall. When we brought it to the house, my ten-year-old son, Elisha, looked in his box and immediately started to pout. I stood back and watched to see how long this was going to go on. Now to many, this might not be a big deal, but when you grew up as I did on a farm, on welfare, and living in a very focused and labor-intensive environment, you gain a great appreciation for never taking the little things in life for granted. I watched my son as passion rose in me to correct his behavior and raise the standard in his life to understand that this is simply not right.

So I said to him, "Elisha, let's go upstairs." Normally this would mean that I was going to discipline him, talk to him, or give him an assignment to write about his actions. But while

I wanted to discipline him, as we walked upstairs I heard the Holy Spirit tell me, "Take him in front of the mirror." So I said, "Elisha, come with me to the bathroom." He looked at me kind of strange, and we walked to the bathroom. We both stood in front of the mirror, and I asked him, "Elisha, what do you see?"

He looked at himself with tears in his eyes, sniffling and crying because he thought he was in trouble. I asked him again, "What do you see?" Still no response, so I told him, "Elisha, why did you start to cry and pout downstairs when you know there are so many children in the world who do not have food?" His eyes brightened. "Elisha, there is no reason for you to have gotten mad or disappointed at your mother and me for not bringing you what you wanted to eat, especially when you texted your mother that what we brought you was the correct thing. You made the mistake in your text, but you want to be mad at us. For what? The reason I brought you up here is to help you understand that the reflection of our lives is not supposed to be about us, but about God and His purpose and plan. We can't live it out based on our standard, but His."

I continued, "It is time to stop being selfish and making everything personal and about you, as God can never get great glory in our lives when all we do is make everything about us. I want you to think about that, son. Do you understand that?"

He responded, "Yes, dad."

"Elisha, I want you to know that the reason I challenge you in areas like this is because God desires to use you mightily because greatness rests on your life, regardless of what you put your hands to. It is His will that we succeed in all we do, but that cannot happen when we make the game of life all about ourselves."

Now this conversation gave me a revelation that, just like my son in this intimate moment we shared, we too sometimes choose to focus only on how the game of life benefits us. However, God's ultimate plan is for us to come outside of ourselves, to raise the standard He has set, so not only is our life impacted, but the lives of all those who are playing alongside us are as well. The outcome of the game of life is not based on our skill or talent, but rather on our ability to be transformed from the image of who we want to be into who God has called us to be. That starts with having a game-winning mentality to trust that if God calls you to play in the game of life, He will also be the one who will guide you in the process of making the right calls that bring Him glory.

CHAPTER 30

MOVING BEYOND YOUR PAST

LIFE CAN BE VERY TOUGH, especially when our perspective is not where it needs to be. We can become so focused on pleasing people, making sure that they are happy, and trying to look the part that we lose ourselves in the process. We can go years focusing more on who others desire for us to become instead of becoming who God has called us to be. If something bad happens to us, we can find ourselves thrown for such a loop that we cannot seem to figure out how to get back to the place where we have peace of mind, body, and spirit. Life is not much different from the game of football, as it too can throw some plays at you that can mess up the entire framework of your perspective.

> **SPIRITUAL TRUTH:** *We are afflicted in every way, but not crushed; perplexed, but not despairing; persecuted, but not forsaken; struck down, but not destroyed; always carrying about in the body the dying of*

Jesus, so that the life of Jesus also may be manifested in our body. (2 Corinthians 4:8)

The amazing thing is that God has placed everything inside of us to make amazing plays in the game of life. We can become paralyzed based on someone else's opinion of who we are, and when this happens we can lose our belief in who we are and base our image of ourselves on someone else's words and not God's. It can become so bad that we forget who we are and start living life based on someone else's perspective, voiding out God's plan and purpose.

Our pasts can seem to have a hold on us, and we find ourselves dwelling on the mistakes we have made. We get stuck and cannot seem to move forward because we can't forgive ourselves. We become so confounded and lost in who we used to be that we cannot even see who God is calling us to be.

SPIRITUAL TRUTH: *'For I know the plans I have for you,' says the LORD. 'They are plans for good and not for disaster, to give you a future and a hope.' (Jeremiah 29:11)*

The outcome of the game of life that we are playing out on a daily basis can be affected by the choices we make and the calls that we allow others to make in our lives. It is extremely important to allow God to become the head coach of our lives.

He has the right to override every bad call that we have made and given others to make.

When I realized that the calls of abuse, alcoholism, womanizing, greed, selfishness, hurt, bitterness, and anger could affect my future in such negative way, I knew it was definitely time to allow God to start being my head coach. That sounds good in theory, but when the game is on the line and you are carrying so many weights of pain that have affected your perspective to see life from a position of hope, most of the time you would rather just continue to play out each day in pain instead of going to a training room of God's word to get some treatment.

For so many years I lived in pain, heartache, and anger, trying to figure out who I was, never giving God a chance because of fear. This is when we all have to look fear in the face and realize we all have played the game of life living outside the boundaries of the rules that God has made. Think about it: Who among us does not have a past? Who hasn't been hurt or knocked down? Who hasn't had a rumor or slander spoken about them? Who hasn't lost a loved one or felt the pain of a broken relationship? Who doesn't have dirty laundry that only God and our intimate confidants know about? Just like the game of football, life can be dirty and treacherous and present some pitfalls, and we can get to a point that when knocked down enough times, it can be very hard to get back up until someone comes along and gives you the right perspective to believe in yourself and who God has called you to be. That is a decision to live life with a purpose-driven mindset, to not allow setbacks to hinder the greater comebacks that God desires to see in our lives. The time is now for all of us to rid ourselves of what has been done, for God has said that He alone knows what plans that He has for us. Plans for us to prosper. To not do us harm and to give us an expectant future, full of His promises. The power that rests in this word is simple.

Each one of us has been given a life to play out, a playbook to follow, and a Head Coach in Jesus Christ as an example and guide on how to play the game of life God's way. But the choice and power of that choice will always rest upon us. We cannot say that we did not know, as it is not God's will that we be unwise. He has come to give us a liberty and freedom to prevail over our past failures. His promise is in us realizing that no matter where we may be in the game of life, there will always be hope, as long as there is a level of expectation that believes in the promise. God's desires for our lives must be independently greater than our own selfish will to not move past our past. We have to see life with a clear focus that God's game plan is 110% greater than our own. He knows that we are more than able to do what He has planned, as long as we are willing to follow what He has placed in front of us. Because even in trial or tribulation, when we are truly committed to the process, there really is nothing that God cannot do in our lives. We have to move out of his way and make room for the greater things that He has in store for us. There is a training that we all must go through in the game of life. As long as we are consistently committed to making Jesus Christ our head coach, we will be able to handle whatever it throws at us. Make the right call.

CHAPTER 31

EVERYONE NEEDS A PLAYBOOK

WITH SO MANY CHOICES to make in the game of life, it is evident that we all need a playbook, a means to guide us through the game of life. There is no doubt that without a playbook, it is very easy to get off course of God's agenda and plan for our lives. With so many choices to make, so many voices to follow, so many circumstances to battle through, and pain from our past to conquer, there is no reason why we do not need a playbook.

Think about your life right now in its current state and reflect on where you are. So many of us choose to call the offensive and defensive moments of our life on our own, hoping for a great outcome in the game of life. In reality, what we are really doing is a trial-by-error offense, hoping that the last call we make will help us advance in the game of life. In reality, God never intended for our lives to be an experiment;

He wants us to apply the wisdom, knowledge, and understanding that rests in the sovereignty of His word to help us learn how to win and play the game of life out His way.

Although we may think that our lives at their current state may be just fine based on the temporal outcome that many see as success, we all must ask ourselves this question: If our lives ended today, what would every person we knew, interacted with, worked with professionally, or were close to as family say about the game plan we are currently using to run our life? Secondly, what would you want them to say?

Are the playbooks and plays of our lives more about what we can gain from this world instead of what we can give to it? Are we more concerned about one more house, one more car, or that one more comma and zero that we can add to our bank account to show the world that we finally made it and are on top?

> **SPIRITUAL TRUTH**: *He saved us, not because of works done by us in righteousness, but according to His own mercy, by the washing of regeneration and renewal of the Holy Spirit, whom He poured out on us richly through Jesus Christ our Savior, so that being justified by His grace we might become heirs according to the hope of eternal life. (Titus 3:5–7)*

As we can see, God's idea of success and ours are two totally different things. Although He has given us the choice of free will to govern our own affairs, there is a set of rules we must live by that helps to guide us in the game of life so that we are living with some boundaries that empower and encourage us toward a life of spiritual growth. These boundaries also provide us with personal discipline, purpose, faithfulness, devotion, hope, peace, understanding, and knowledge, and a game plan that is totally committed to Jesus Christ helping us make the right calls. Although my playbook may have gotten me through the first quarter of my life, it could not keep me on God's path, simply because my idea of calling my own plays in life was never by God's design to work. This is why he sent Jesus Christ to be an example of a real player in the game of life who could teach us that how we are calling the game is wrong.

It took me examining where I was, seeing the dysfunctional state of my mind, and allowing God to transform, renew, and restore a heart of victory to focus on playing the game of life by a whole new set of rules.

Part of that process I learned was from playing the game of football, but more importantly from making one bad mistake after another until the game of life got hard enough to finally help me realize that these lessons, although tough, were there for a greater purpose. If I was going to make any progress moving forward, I was going to have to embrace the process of being coached by God. Now He would be my coach, just like many of the coaches I had in football who had taught me how to play the game I loved. Now it was my time to fall in love with the game of life and allow God to show me how to embrace the power that comes through change. I had to stop thinking that the mindset I took to create most of the problems I had would be the same one that would help solve them. I had to allow God to create in me a new heart, a right mind and spirit to move forward in His will over my own. Like so many of my coaches who had taught me lessons over the years, there was always one common goal: to win, but this time in life.

Now every coach I have ever had, regardless of who they were—whether it was Phil Senter, John Philips, Mack Brown, Carl Torbush, Rich Kotite, Norv Turner, Marty Schotteinheimer, Marvin Lewis, Steve Spurrier, Lovie Smith, or Tony Dungy—had a knack just at the right moment of finding that one play that could make the biggest impact and difference on me understanding how to play my position, but more importantly, on how to play the game. They were not just interested in me getting better, but learning how my play could impact the greater good of our team. Even in the midst of winning and sometimes losing, they taught me invaluable lessons in both. The process from every great coach was always the same: Identify the error, correct the mistake, apply wisdom on how to do it right, then go out there and perform it to the best of your God-given ability.

To be honest, although the Lord's infinite wisdom con-founds our minds, his approach is simplistic and somewhat the same. God's ultimate playbook teaches us to identify the character flaws we have in life, address the pain, deal with the panic and anxiety, deal with confusion, identify areas of hurt, and embrace the power healing. We learn to grow in the faith, truth, and love that lives in salvation in Jesus Christ; to trust in God, move into destiny and purpose, and keep our eyes focused on what is ahead and not behind. Because God knows that as long as we live our lives based on where we were instead of who He has called us to be, we will never make progress.

EDDIE MASON

...originally from Siler City, North Carolina, is a former American football linebacker in the National Football League. He played for the New York Jets, the Jacksonville Jaguars and the Washington Redskins. Previously, he played college football at the University of North Carolina, and was drafted into professional football in the sixth round of the 1995 NFL draft.

After a shoulder injury forced him to retire, Mason decided to hold a sports camp for kids. Seeing the positive impact that a combination of athletic and spiritual training had, in 2004, he opened a training program and gym in Sterling, Virginia, under the name MASE Training Sports Performance & Fitness Center. Playing off Mason's nickname, MASE is an acronym for Muscle and Spiritual Empowerment. At the 7,500-square-foot, two-floor facility, he and other trainers serve a clientele base made up of grade school, junior high and high school students, stay-at-home moms, CEOs, college football players, and current and former Washington Redskins players.